SHUT UP!
BE A "DAMN" MAN!

RICHARD E BLAKE

SHUT UP! BE A "DAMN" MAN

Bennett books may be ordered through booksellers or by contacting:

Bennett Media and Marketing
1603 Capitol Ave., Suite 310 A233
Cheyenne, WY 82001
www.thebennettmediaandmarketing.com
Phone: 1-307-202-9292

ISBN: 978-1-957114-32-3 (Paperback)
ISBN: 978-1-957114-33-0 (eBook)

Printed in the United States of America

Bennett Media rev. date: 07/29/2022

TABLE OF CONTENTS

To the Almighty God. To all the men affected by silent effects of sexual abuse and to those men that had an impact on me throughout my life. To Raymond Underwood (Sleep in Peace).

PREFACE

This book is about the profound impact on a male child that sexual abuse by a female can cause.

Acknowledgments

To my children, siblings, editor/publisher, Jeff Jones, and Pastor Timothy Veal.

CHAPTER 1

THE BASTARD CHILD

This first chapter is an eye-opener about the relationship between my father and me, which occurred before, during, and after I was sexually abused. I really can't remember when the verbal abuse by my father started or even why it started. All I do know is that as long as I could recall, my father's nickname for me was bastard.

"Do this, you bastard."

"Stop that, you bastard."

I really thought my name was bastard instead of my given name, which was Richard. And some- times his disgust and anger of whatever it was that made him despise me would be followed by a hard kick in the butt, and if he missed his target, his foot would land in the small of my back.

Now the house we lived in was a small brown duplex and was built for the use of two families, and we could only play in the front because the back was a weeded area, which covered the left over trash that was thrown there by the tenants who refused to take the trash to the collection site. So we were forbidden to use that area. I remember one particular day, I was caught behind the house, sitting on the ground, because I was too ashamed to play in front with the other children. I don't know how old I was, but I do remember sitting there in a world of my own, enjoying the peace and the warmth of the sunshine, thinking about why I was so different from the other children, who were laughing and having a good time.

Anyway, on this particular day, my father pulled up and had another person in the car. It happened to be his brother, my uncle from Chicago, whom I had never seen before. I knew all my mother's siblings but only my aunts on my dad's side. As the day went on, we began to relax as my sister and brother and I got to know him, because he was a funny-acting man about forty years of age and he made us laugh.

Later on that night (I knew it was night because it was dark outside and the street lights were on), my uncle either asked me to do something or reply to his question, and whatever it was, I was too slow in responding. To my surprise, he lifted his foot and kicked me, just as my father would do. I began to cry out for my father, but he acted like it did not even happen, so I became very angry and started to cuss him for all it was worth (in my mind, of course). I remember picking up my toy fire truck and slinging it at him. He tried to defend himself because the truck was made of metal and if he was struck, he would receive a nasty cut.

Needless to say, I received one of the worst butt kicking from my father I've ever had, and even though he had disciplined me many times before, along with the physical and verbal abuse, I still respected him and did everything I could to please him. This was a day like no other, and my respect turned into hate, which was not hard, being that I never truly loved him. But I spent a lot of my life trying to please him, and it made me angry that he was never satisfied with anything I tried to do (which we will discover as I continue to write).

But it was at this time that I began to form my own opinion about the so-called grown-ups and their idea of raising children and developed blatant disrespect for authority. And the real sad part about it was, I had not reached school age yet. I had not even started kindergarten, and already I was set to fail.

This all happened while we were living in the brown duplex, and I had one of the most frightful encounters with a woman I'll just call Miss Pretty Sneaky Smile.

CHAPTER 2

ABUSED BY A WOMAN

I first met Miss Pretty Sneaky Smile during the time my parents had decided they had had enough of paying rent. Even though the rent was affordable, the living conditions were not up to par. We were contending with the field mice that had access to the apartment at will, and rats were always around the sites for trash, which were also collected at will—sometimes every two weeks and some-times once a month.

In any event, they both decided that it was time to say goodbye to the brown duplex and move to a better part of the city, as did a few other families. But before they moved, I guess my father needed my mother to go to work so they would have a nice down payment even though at the time I didn't know whether they were buying a home or would continue to rent somewhere else. My assessment of the situation came after having to go through the same process when I decided to buy my first home some thirty years or more later.

But in the process, Mom went to work for these rich white folks as a housekeeper, which in those days consisted of being the maid and the babysitter. So in the meantime, Mom needed a babysitter for her own three children, who were not yet of school age (or at least two of us were not). Maybe my oldest sister might have been since she was almost two years older than I.

But I remember my mother introducing this very young lady to my sister and me and giving us instructions on how we should act and that it was important that we gave her the upmost respect. I can remember looking up at her with that pretty smile. At that time, it was a smile of happiness and joy and laughter but would later turn into the most damaging and frightful times in my young life.

Again I will never know how or why this abuse came about or what I did to initiate the start of this action or what made her choose me to carry out these heinous acts on. After all, I was only four or five years of age and still couldn't remember attending any school. And it was only later in my life, through many abusive acts of my own, that I realized she had to have suffered abuse in her life as well.

It began on a summer day, and my sister and I were preparing to go outside and play, which was something I very rarely did. She opened the front door, and as my sister and I started to bolt out the door, she grabbed me by my arm and said, "Buddy [which was the nickname my father had given me, although at times I think he himself had forgotten], I want you to stay inside with me," which was not a hard choice for me since I was just as comfortable staying inside, playing with my toys.

But on this particular day, Miss Pretty Sneaky Smile had something else in mind. She closed the front door and went to the closet and opened the door and instructed me to go in. Now I'm not in the habit of liking being in the dark, but since she was already in there, I thought I would be safe. But what she made me do would change my life as a child and catapult me into a lifestyle filled with confusion, conflict, and hate.

I can't remember how many times she made me perform this act in the span of her babysitting job, but it was enough to turn me into a sexual monster. I can't even remember penetrating her, but I remember she liked me to perform oral sex. And the scary thing about it was the big wad of hair I would have to go through to perform and to satisfy her, and she always had a washcloth to wash away the evidence.

And I can still hear her saying, "Now, Buddy, don't you tell nobody." And I didn't. For one reason, I was ashamed, and for another reason, I felt my father would punish me for everything that went on. It would justify that name bastard, which he called me.

Like I said, I don't know how long this went on, but it went from something being scary to something I liked, and I started looking forward to having those sessions in the closet with her.

But it all ended after we moved, and it was then I knew I was scarred for life. Although it would be some years before I would have a sexual encounter, the dreams and the fantasies would continue. I had dreams of sexual encounters with anybody and everybody. And only a few people knew the name of this woman, because I vowed to never tell for a number of reasons—one, because since that time she has passed away (and, I hope, is in heaven) and, two, because she had children my age and I would never embarrass them. We all grew up together and remain friends to this day.

This book is not about hurting or condemning but is about the effects abuse can have on a male child, and I hope it will convince a young man to seek help if they have suffered abuse from a female or any other person and also that it will alert parents that while the female child is somewhat protected, the male child is left primarily on his own.

My mom continued to work for some years after we moved into our own home, which she and my dad did purchase. I had several more babysitters, but there were none like Ms. Pretty Sneaky Smile, who, unbeknownst to me, would shape my life to come—sometimes in a good way but mostly in a way that over the years would cause me to become a confused young man, both physically and mentally. Not only did she cause me to form a low and trashy opinion of women, but I would not hesitate to verbally and sometimes physically abuse them also. And I would find out later in life that it is one of the worst things a man can become.

Also over the years, I formed an even lower opinion of gay men, and even though I had met them in social settings, I was never enticed to go in that direction because I could never figure out why they wanted to be or represent a human being of such disgust. And as the years began to fly by, I would find myself in situations that up until God began to show me as He cleansed me spiritually, I could not understand. I could not see past my guilt and shame, so I carried like them like yokes of slavery (Galatians 5:1).

CHAPTER 3

MY SCHOOL YEARS

As I stated earlier, the years began to gently go by as I entered my school years. These were the years when I began to really see the effect of my childhood abuse, both by my father and the babysitter. They both abused me in different ways, but both ended in the same results.

Now this next chapter probably is the shortest chapter of the book but is the most compelling. I was alerted that something was wrong in my life, and the most stressful part was the fact that, at a young age, I had experienced perhaps more than all my peers and those that were responsible for giving me positive directions in my life did not know that being positive had already been basically destroyed before I knew what the word *positive* meant.

I remember my first day of school. I was actually scared out of my wits. I was in the midst of people that I had no desire to be around. At that time, when integration had not yet come about, I found myself in a school that was fully integrated, and you could tell it was a new process to the black children as well as the white.

I remember my first day of school. I was actually scared out of my wits. I was in the midst of people that I had no desire to be around. At that time, when integration had not yet come about, I found myself in a school that was fully integrated, and you could tell it was a new process to the black children as well as the white.

The white students gravitated toward one another, and the black students gravitated to their kind. Now that I have gotten older, I realized, what else could they be expected to do as they were thrust in the middle of grown folks' problems, which they had no idea how to solve? We were expected to get along with one another when most of us were taught we were mortal enemies. We were thrown in the midst of grown folks' hatred and expected to get an education.

But in any case, I found myself not wanting to be bothered with any side, because I carried a secret that was deeper than they could not imagine (or so I thought).

In any case, I entered my kindergarten class with apprehension. I remember wanting to go to the restroom so badly, and if it were not for a teacher recognizing the distress on my face, I would have wet my pants. Then after getting to the bathroom door, I almost did not go in because it took me back to the closet, but after I went in and discovered how big it was, I thought, *What a wonderful place to hide!* And this led to my first encounter with breaking a school rule—no loitering in restrooms. The sign was clearly there, but I could not understand it since I could not read.

So after I was pulled by my ear to the classroom, I got a sense of who was in authority, and none of them looked like me or my mother or father, not even the pastor of the church I went—and I thought He had absolute authority. But again, I quickly adjusted and sat on the quilt that was laid on the floor and began to listen to the teacher go over the proverbial ABCs (otherwise known as the alphabet). So my education began, but it was second to the education I had already been taught.

Nevertheless, I began to somewhat enjoy the singing and playtime. Recess was my favorite, although I didn't play much. I would find myself daydreaming or asleep. One of the best parts of those days was, among all the people that would become my friends were these two little white girls (twins) who, for some reason, wanted me to sit between them. And for some reason, they could keep my mind off my dirty little thoughts, which usually plagued me constantly. Even though they were girls, they presented an innocence that I did not find in the girls of my own race, and until this day, I have not had any desire to have sex with white women, although I have fantasized seeing their private parts, to see if theirs looked like those of women of color. Plus, I was told they smelled like dogs so that within itself was a turnoff (racism at its best).

But as time went on, I learned to adjust to the school system, which was totally biased and prejudiced against people of color, and that added fuel to the fire of an already-disturbed mind. My dislike for white people caused me not to be interested in white girls, and on top of that, I was afraid to talk to them or any other girl my age because for that matter, I always thought they could read my mind and could feel what I had experienced and looked at me differently from the boys, whom I thought was much dumber than the girls at school.

Now it must have been around the fourth or fifth grade that the most ironic thing happened and would kind of curtail my dislike toward white people in a most unusual way. I was walking home late from school because I had to stay over for some reason (which I can't quite remember now), maybe either for fighting or for not obeying the teacher. But on the eleventh block on my walk home (I walked because we had no school buses at that time, at least in our neighborhood), I came upon a white boy crying and sobbing profusely and complaining about how he was treated by the black students while on his way home.

I don't know why I was even concerned about this boy's problems, but I began to question him, only to find he had a speech impediment and wore unusually thick glasses, which was enough to make you laugh. I quickly understood his dilemma, but for some reason, which I could not understand at the time, God was teaching me my first real-life lesson about friendship.

Now while I'm not calling out too many names in my book, I have to tell you his name. It was George Washington Ludlow; his family was a carryover in the neighborhood, one of the last remaining white families still residing in the area, which was quickly becoming predominantly black. Whites were moving out as fast as blacks were moving in.

Anyhow, George and I became friends, and I somehow, unbeknownst to me, became his protection, like a bodyguard. I can't tell you from the fourth to around the sixth grade how many black eyes, busted lips, and swollen jaws I got taking up for George. And after we got to his house, sometimes at full speed, he would run into the house and bring me the biggest piece of candy I'd ever seen (at least it was at that time). It would either be an Almond Joy or a Mounds bar. Even though his parents rejected our friendship, George was not hearing it, and he did it almost daily until his family moved out of the neighborhood.

Again as time rolled by, my next face-to-face meeting with my issue came in the seventh grade. I call this my first love. I remember her so well because she was the most beautiful girl in the entire school. She had the most perfect smile and had the most wonderful, outgoing personality (or so I thought), and the most important thing of all, she seemed to like me!

But my analogical past rose again. I was so afraid to get close to her because of my sexual experiences. I didn't know if I loved her, but I sure did like her a lot. We would talk and laugh, but I would never go past that point—no kiss on the cheek or touching hands or walks from school, like many of the other kids did. I was so afraid she would discover my past. And I didn't want to ruin the relationship we had, because I respected her so much that what we had was good enough for me at that time. This went on for a whole school year. Then our relationship (if you could call it that) came to an abrupt halt when two brothers moved to our city from down South. One of the brothers, whose name I won't mention, was quite handsome and slightly bowlegged, and all the girls went bonkers over him. Anyway, he ended up stealing my girl. He got her pregnant, and her family moved to California. Needless to say, my trust in women, which I had very little of, declined to an even lower level.

And even though the young man ended up marrying another beautiful girl, she ended up his worst nightmare, and it ended in two children and a divorce. I would always say that it was payback for stealing my girl, but later I realized it was my fear of my past that caused me to lose her. I did see her years later in California. We only spoke briefly, as we both had moved on. I had enlisted in the Marine Corps, and she was married herself.

Needless to say, although I stayed in trouble, I was at least an average student. I played basketball in the eighth grade, didn't like to practice, and quit the team. I went out for football in the ninth grade, and after I made the team, I walked proudly home in my football uniform to show my father. When I got home, he was sitting on the porch and, with a look of disgust on his face, told me I looked like a fool. Needless to say, that ended my football career. Not only did that end my football career, but it ended my desire to go to school. I began to hang out with the older dropouts and pick up really bad habits, such as drinking and smoking. But I discovered one good thing about myself. I had a pretty good singing voice. I think I was about thirteen, and I knew at that point that I wanted to be a singer and also why I liked music class. For that reason, I went back to school, but in order for me to return, I had to repeat the ninth grade, where my younger brother was in. That made me feel like Lioness on Dennis the Menace, so it wasn't long before I was out again. In the meantime, I heard a group of men singing one day in a neighbor's house, and it sounded good, so I went to their house and heard the most beautiful sound I had ever heard. Now I knew about the church choir and liked singing oldies with the dropouts, but this was a spiritual sound that I had never heard before, and I knew I wanted to be a part of that sound. And since it was a neighbor's house, I didn't think my father, who was an elder in the church, would mind. They welcomed me and another dropout friend into the group. And they traveled on the weekend to other cities to sing—such as Chicago and Gary. It suited me just fine; that was right up my alley.

Now the neighbor's name was Mr. Cleo. He took me under his wing and taught me the musical scale and different notes. He became like a second father to me. Plus, his sons and I went to school together, so everything was working out—until my father found out they were Baptist. Although he never said much, I could tell he was displeased.

After about a year of traveling and singing on the radio, I became a town celebrity and was also the youngest lead singer in most of the groups that were around, including most of the famous groups still singing today. And my father came to hear me at least twice in that whole year. It might have been longer. One time, he came, and I began to cry because I thought I was finally doing something to please him. But I found out later he came to see if I could really sing. It came naturally to me because he and my mother had pretty good voices themselves.

In the midst of all the confusion, I found a girlfriend who was around eighteen, and I had not yet turned fifteen. She was also pregnant by another man, but I somehow did not care. We dated until she had her baby, and I pretended it was mine and became very protective of him. Even at my age, I treated him like my son because I didn't want him to be treated like I was, growing up. After she had the baby, we began to have sex quite often, and it was then I discovered I liked older women because that was my very first sexual encounter. I didn't have to hide who and what I had become. Also it kept me from trying to look up under the schoolteacher's dress. I had done so many times and fantasized about a sexual encounter with her.

Again time slid by, and my dad and I had one more man-to-man encounter. This time, it was almost to the death. I had a baseball bat, and needless to say, he had hid a pistol up his sleeve. I guess someone in the neighborhood called the police, and they threatened to take me to jail and gave me a choice to join the military, if my parents would agree. My dad happily agreed, and my mother thought it was best for me also. At that time, all the neighborhood young men were joining the Marines, so that was where I wanted to go. So off to Chicago I went, I somehow passed the test, and off to boot camp I went—at the ripe old age of fifteen.

CHAPTER 4

MILITARY EXPERIENCE

So on October 24, 1962, after a long debate with myself and whether I made the right choice or not, I found myself at the famous Marine boot camp site in Paris Island, South Carolina. I was being rushed through the indoctrination, and most of that first day was a living hell. I kept wondering if my immaturity was showing because most of the other recruits were two to three years my senior and had graduated either from high school or military school. To answer the question, yes, it was. It was then that I found out I was not as much of a man as I thought I was. It was then that I found out that the sexual abuse by the babysitter and the verbal and physical abuse by my father were more to do with anger, hatred, and shame rather than manhood.

Nothing I had ever gone through prepared me for the experiences I was about to face. Besides the rigorous training, I found myself having to do something that I always had trouble with, and that was obeying those that had authority over me, including my father. From the second day, when the drill instructors woke us up a 3:00 a.m., I said to myself, *Houston, we have a problem!* I had no problem with the physical training (or PT, as they called it) or even the history lessons about the corps because that was why I joined the Marines. It was the best, and the most elite branch of service for me. But the big problem to me was, I was the only black recruit in my platoon. The only other time I was the only black in something was when my mother dropped me off at a new school that had just been finished, and the school system wanted to integrate it, so they started with me. I was so afraid I wet my pants. Plus, my mother left me standing in the hallway, and I was left there for what seemed like hours before I was taken to class.

Also the N-word in those days was tossed around like seeds on a plantation. Now in school if someone called me the N-word, the fight was on, and although I was called a troublemaker by the whites, the blacks said the same thing, which made me angry because they seemed not to want to stand up for themselves. But now here I was in the midst of all these seemingly big white giants, alone. I was the only black in the entire platoon, and after experiencing the time I was the only black in an entire school, that feeling of having to stand up for myself by myself came over me again, and the wall of protection began to rebuild itself.

I remember my first encounter with the recruit that was appointed as the platoon guide and was usually in charge of cleaning our barracks where we lived. He was from Boston and had graduated from OCS (officer candidate) school. He had red hair and was meaner than two junkyard dogs and lived up to the place where he came from. He was a pure racist and didn't care who knew it. Anyway, he would never say the N-word out loud but would get in my ear and say it when he gave me my cleaning duties, which was usually cleaning the head (restrooms) with a toothbrush. On one particular day, as I was scrubbing the floor, he used the N-word, and I thought I had proven to myself and others that I had a thick skin and had had enough of his abuse. Plus even though he was white and redheaded, he reminded me of my father. I threw the water in his face and commenced to beat him profusely about the head and shoulders with the mop bucket. Needless to say, I was found guilty of insubordination and sent on a two-week stay in a special platoon they called Motivation. I guess I was to be reprogramed. That was a place where they sent recruits who found it hard to adjust to military life.

Well, after about a week, I was sent back to my platoon with a letter from the company commander that said they found me to be very intelligent and they could see no reason I was there in the first place. Needless to say, I went on to graduate and was sent to Camp Lejeune, North Carolina, for the next leg of my military experience.

At Camp Lejeune, it was mostly camping out, hikes, and military tactics, which I loved because it took me away from all the thoughts of my past life as a civilian. I had a home that as long as I wanted to stay was mine, and I wanted to make a career out of my military life. I could feel the pressures of the past being lifted off my shoulders, but little did I know I would come face-to-face with it again.

Then after my infantry training, I was transferred to Camp Pendleton in sunny California, which would become perhaps the most eventful time in my life. I had been in only one big city, and that was Chicago. It was nothing compared to San Diego or Los Angles. The excitement was overwhelming, and the pace of everyday living was three times as fast. People were different, and it had a no-holds-barred atmosphere. I quickly learned that if you didn't keep up, you would be lost in the shuffle.

I was at the tender age of seventeen, and I would turn eighteen in January. It was only September. The weather was hot in the daytime and almost cold at night, so I quickly caught the worst case of the flu I've had ever had. Needless to say, my first two weeks were spent on the base, getting acclimated to the crazy weather, which confused the term "sunny California." The time zone change didn't help either.

After weathering the storm, so to speak, and between the training and the inspections, which seemed twice a week, I finally got a chance to get off base. I had two choices—the city of San Diego or LA. I chose San Diego because you could go across the border to Mexico from there, and I thought that was great—I could just walk into another country. And my plan was to really enjoy my three-day weekend.

Now I knew very little about prostitutes, and the little sex that I had experienced was a two-way street. Whatever was done was for the enjoyment of both of us. Here I was in the middle of all the sex I could handle, and I was scared to death. Although there were some beautiful women, sex to me was making love, which included oral sex, and I was not going to go down on these women who had been with a man every fifteen minutes (sometimes it seemed quicker than that). I found no pleasure in that. Plus, I was not going to catch anything I could not get rid of, so since I could not enter most nightclubs or bars in the US, I had to find another way for sexual pleasure.

I would spend the next month residing on the base while the rest of the guys, who mostly were older than I was, seemed more outgoing. Plus I was trying to hide what my past abuse had made me. So I would sit alone, like I did most of my young life, and sometimes cry over what I missed as a child and found no joy and excitement in this life I chose, which all the other guys found so much fun in.

So this life I thought would give me a sense of freedom and relief from all my issues seemed to weigh heavily on my mind that I thought of just leaving and going AWOL, which would lead to a dishonorable discharge, and I would be done with it. Plus I knew I was too much of a coward to commit suicide. You've heard of people suffering from post-traumatic stress when they leave the military; I think I had it coming in.

Then I would think about my mom and all the times she would come to my rescue when I was in my depressed state of mind and would hear her say, "Now, Buddy, get up from there and do something with your life. It's not over yet. The good will come."

One day, I was going to go out to one of the clubs for enlisted men, which was on the base. I could go in but could not drink. Plus, they had good food aside from the food we ate on an everyday basis. I sat down beside an old sergeant. At least at that time, I thought he was old. I found out later he was only thirty-five, but we began to talk, and I asked him why he was still in the base and not out having a good time. He replied his joy was making money and that when he went out, he had a special lady he would go see. I thought to myself, *Wow, that sounds like something I would be interested in.* I found out he was a loan shark (if you want to call it that), but he would loan money to all the men that went out every weekend and was broke before payday, which was once a month. He would charge 25 percent on the dollar, and since I spent a lot of time on the base, that seemed like something I could get into (or so I thought).

I quickly found out you had to be a special kind of person to be a loan shark in the military. First, it was against the military code to lend money for interest, and if you got caught, you'd be in trouble. Most of the time, it ended up in paying a fine. My friend was a sergeant, and I was a private making $78 a month and was sending $50 of that back home for my mother to save until I got out in four years.

Nevertheless, I was successful at this newfound scheme and did it for a good while, but I found out you had to really be on top of your game because you were lending money to men who were not too responsible. I would sometimes end up in a brawl to get my money back, and sometimes I would only break even. But I was okay with that and was ready to take the next step in finding me a lady to see off the base.

By this time, I had turned eighteen and was really smelling myself, so a friend invited to a party in San Diego, and that was all I needed. I went to the party, and I met a woman there. I knew she was older than me, and that was fine because I knew she was experienced. I could let my hair down with her again, or so I thought. Anyway, she invited me over to her apartment, and I spent the night there—no sex because she knew I was younger than her and she was not about to have sex with a child. Plus, she was thirty-two, and I had lied and told her I was twenty-two (at least, I was over twenty one).

Anyway, back to the base my friend and I went, and I had no sex. My friend kept drilling me to see if I had had sex with her, almost as if he was interested in her himself. Of course, I lied, thinking that would deter his interest in her. This was on a Sunday, and we had a weeklong military maneuver coming up. That meant a week in the boondocks, so I had to prepare for that and would not have time to write her as I had planned.

Needless to say, we did end up having sex, and it was everything I wanted it to be. I actually found myself in love with her, and she ended up getting pregnant, which almost destroyed her because she found out my real age. I remember her saying she was having a baby by a baby, and she wanted to get rid of it by taking quinine pills. I begged her not to, that I might be young but I was man enough to help her take care of our child. And then another dilemma came up. We were scheduled to go overseas, and I don't know to this day what happened to her, whether she had the baby or not. She called my company commander to stop me from going to Okinawa, but I remember him scolding her about getting pregnant by a child and that she could get in trouble from the authorities. Even though I wanted to stay with her, I also wanted to go overseas, so off to Okinawa I went.

Just before we left Camp Pendleton, rumors were flying around about the Vietnam conflict, and that we might be headed that way after our cold-weather training in Japan. Everybody was kind of at a period of mixed emotions. Some were hoping they could show off their training, and others were thinking about their families. To me, it was just another adventure that I was looking forward to. It helped keep my mind off my past, and at that point in my life, I was not afraid of death even though I was nervous about someone shooting back at me.

But we packed our gear and boarded the big C-130 Hercules for the eighteen-hour flight to Japan. As I sat in the thin-canvas seats, I wondered how we were going to be in the air for that long. And I did have sense enough to say a prayer for God to keep us in the air without any trouble. I think I slept most of the way. I think most of us troops were thinking the same thing: "If we go down, let me be sleep."

Thank God we made a safe landing at the airstrip about twelve that night. It was common practice to always land at night as a safety measure against any kind of attack from the enemy. We got our gear and were loaded on six-by's, which were the names of the military vehicles used to transport us to the base. It was called Camp Hansen, and later, we were transferred to another base called Camp Swab.

About a month after arriving, we were permitted our first liberty call into Okinawa, and everyone seemed to be excited and were questioning the old-timers on where to go to have a good time. That was when I found out that racism was alive and well even in an outfit with a great history, like the Marine Corps. The white soldiers went to a city called Kadena, and the black soldiers went to the place called the Four Corners, which was the poorest part of Okinawa. The ironic thing was, the whites could go to where we were and hang out, but if we went to where they hung out, the MPs would chase us away. Sometimes we would get arrested. Needless to say, that did not sit too well with me, especially in my state of mind.

If it had not been for my friends that pushed me into going, I would have stayed on the base. Most of them came through boot camp and ITR with me, so I reluctantly came along. So we piled into the small cabs that were meant for no more than four people. We would have six or seven in a car, and the driver would haul ass around the mountains as fast as that little car would go. We had no idea how much danger we were in.

The closer we came to the Four Corners, the more I regretted coming. It was that same feeling that I felt when I visited Tijuana, Mexico. How could I enjoy sex with it just being satisfaction for me? But I quickly decided that I would find a way to enjoy myself. After we got into the city and I smelled how foul it smelled of urine and garbage, I again became depressed. But as the night went on and the drinks became stronger, I went into one of the little shacks and got pleasured. Then I came to the conclusion that was all I needed, and I headed back to the base.

As time went on, we found out that the Vietnam rumors were true and we would be the first to see action. Some were gung ho, and others were silent, in their opinion. Although I was not a good garrison soldier in the field, I was untouchable, so I was picked to be one of a hundred soldiers for special training by the Navy SEAL in what was later named the amphibious raid team. We were given submarine training and amphibious raid training, which I enjoyed very much. For the first time since I joined, I felt important being a part of the first of such a unit. I understand it is now a normal part of the Marines.

I thank God for my tours in Vietnam. It was a special place to me. I fell in love for the first time there, even though the girl and I never met. She was a beautiful young lady whom I saw while on guard duty one day. She was watching me through the barbed-wire fence. I really didn't know how long she had been watching me and didn't know why. I think it was maybe because I looked so much younger than the rest of the soldiers she saw on guard duty. When I looked up and saw how beautiful she was, I immediately tried to communicate with her, but she spoke no English. Somehow she really stole my heart. She would sometimes switch to speaking French, and that would really make me want her. She would always be there when I had guard duty. I never found out how she knew what days or time I would be at that guard station, but somehow she knew.

Even though I was stung by (to this day) the biggest wasp I have ever seen, bitten on my private part by a field mouse, and ran upon a python, I still loved Vietnam. They called me Ricky Son. I could walk to any village by myself. I learned from the people and respected them, and they respected me. When it was time to leave and I was ready to come home, I still felt sad. Even though I lost friends and saw my comrades die and lose body parts, I knew somehow we had no reason to be there. I remember when the then senator John Kerry spoke out against some of the atrocities committed by the US soldiers against the people of Vietnam, they called him a liar. But I was a witness. I stood in front of a Vietnamese woman to stop a soldier from killing her while we raided her village. I soon learned that war brings out the real personality in a person. Some were passionate, some were sturdy and strong, and then there were those that disguised their hatred and evil ways to the point where taking a life was the best part of the job. But in any case, lives were lost no matter how we perceived our reason for being there.

And it had a profound impact on me since I was already suffering from my own issues and knowing I was on my way back home to a place that didn't regard me as an equal, even after I had served my country with honor.

CHAPTER 5

RETURNING STATESIDE

I could never forget the day we got orders to evacuate from our post. We prepared to get on a ship going to Japan (or so we thought), but at twelve o'clock that night, for some reason, we slid out under the cover of darkness. I found out later that our government did not want the North Vietnamese to think we were retreating; instead they wanted them to think we were just using military tactics. Nevertheless, we said our goodbyes, and to our surprise, we boarded what was called an LCM, which was a small vessel used to bring combat soldiers and supplies to the shore. We had not used it before because we were dropped from helicopters. Although we had been trained for them, we never used them while we were in combat.

Now mind you, these were flat-bottom boats, and we were going across the Sea of Japan. To my understanding, this is the roughest body of water you will ever encounter. Plus, we were crossing right in the middle of typhoon season, and we were right in the midst of one that night. The farther we got out to sea, the worse it got. Now if you have never been in a flat-bottom boat riding on twelve-foot waves, then you have no idea what I am talking about. The waves would roll under the boat, and before the next wave came, it would fall like a ton of bricks back down to sea level and would raise us up again on the next wave. We rode the waves for about nine hours of that; add in the smell of diesel fuel, and we were plenty high and sick.

The storm tore off the tops of some of the boats and destroyed the communications, so there was no way to radio for help in case one or more of the boats capsized. There was no way to rescue anyone. But thank God we rode out the storm. Things began to settle down, and my mind began to take me back to where it left me before we left the shores of Vietnam.

Even with all that I had been through—the deaths, the loss of limbs, the hurt and the pain, and the suffering of others—I still ended up thinking about the issues I had to face within myself. That's the thing about any kind of abuse. No matter what you encounter in life, no matter how bad the situation gets, it seems to somehow take over and dominate everything you have experienced. It always finds its way to the top, like cream in milk. Even when you think you have forgotten it, it reminds you that it controls your very being.

It reminds you that whatever you go through or suffer with, it only enhances its ugliness and increases the shame you carry. Even if you think you have accomplished something meaningful, it lets you know that you will never be good enough. It will destroy every good thing you try to do and every good relationship you try to have. And it lets you know that the only place you will fit in is with those that felt like you, if there was any indication, because there were no signs.

I often wondered why God allowed me to live. I would be close to death, but somehow he would protect me even when it looked for sure I was a goner. Once, we were on R and R (rest and relaxation), and all my comrades wanted to go to Thailand, but I wanted to go to Bangkok. They left and had to take a C-130 flight out of the Hong Kong harbor, but the whole plane blew up as it was taking off. I lost all my friends but one, and the funny thing was, they fished him out of the sea. He had never swam a day in his life, but he swam underwater to escape the gas burning on the surface of the water. I thought to myself, *Would I have been so lucky?*

Even when I was in combat and returned to the compound, I would never write my mother a letter, because if anything happened, I didn't want her to worry. No one would ever know about the baggage I was carrying around and how afraid I was of having a normal life with a wife and kids and how damaged I was inside.

But somehow she got a letter to my captain, and he ordered me to write. I lied to her and said I was fine and that everything was good. I was on my way home and would see her in a couple of months. When I got back to the States, I never wanted her to know what I was going through. But if I told her, she would feel guilty and blame herself, and I didn't want that. So there was no one else to tell, especially another man. They surely would not understand, because most would think being sexually abused by a woman was a badge of honor, like my brothers did.

I never could understand at that time why of all the things I had been through after joining the service, I still could not shake this feeling of shame and guilt from something that happened to me so early in my life. Why was God, who talked about forgetting the past and moving forward, keep sending me back to the beginning of my life, to things I wanted to forget? I wanted to move forward. But what was His purpose?

Even through the drinking and the drugs and all the other activities that I would indulge in, such as attending church and going to charity events, which I thought somehow would purge me of the filthiness I carried inside, I would experience these feelings. But I managed to gather my thoughts well enough to think that going back home would somehow heal me of my past. I had a less than a year left on a four-year term that actually ended up being five because of bad times. I had to make up for different non-serious offenses that I had committed throughout my service duties.

Nevertheless, I figured once I got back to the good old US of A, I could start my life over. At that time, I contemplated getting married. I thought that somehow marriage would help heal me because at least my wife would fill the desires of my sexual habits and having a job and having children to protect would be the answer to my problem. But as you will see after reading on, that was the worst scenario I could have come up with. What was I thinking? Why would I think I could do this without professional help? At that time, I had nowhere to seek it from. I went into the military at fifteen, and even after five years, I still had not reached drinking age. I felt I was well into my manhood and could handle whatever life had to offer.

I remember well the day we again boarded the C-130 Hercules transport planes from Okinawa to Camp Pendleton, California. We landed twelve hours later in California on a bright and sunny day. We proceeded by truck to the parade field and was given leave right at that spot, which to me was a wonderful idea since like many others I had filled my seabag half with clothing and the other half with some of that good Vietnam grass, which we had gotten accustomed to and could not leave behind. The women and the children came secondary to the marijuana we loved.

From California, I decided to go home and see my mother and father—mostly, Mom. I had new brothers and sisters I had not yet met. Plus, my younger brother who was also in the military was home at the same time. He was one of the first African Americans to finish West Point Military Academy, and I was very proud of him because he himself had overcome a lot of adversity to achieve what he had achieved. Being a lieutenant, I could not wait to salute him.

But knowing I was the cock of the walk, so to speak, and having served in combat and earned some ribbons and medals, I was pretty proud of myself and was happy with myself even in my state of mind. Well, after seeing my father and the expression on his face, my proudness was short-lived, and somehow I felt he was jealous for some reason. I found out he had been in WWI, and at that time, blacks only served as cooks or domestic help. So after a heated exchange and fifteen days into a thirty-day leave, I said my goodbyes and headed to my next duty station—Camp Lejeune, North Carolina.

I arrived at Camp Lejeune on a Saturday. I remember so well because it was kind of a brisk and windy day and was kind of cool for that time of year. The base was like a deserted town, and I already figured out there must be plenty to do and places to go in the surrounding cities. There was usually plenty of happenings in the service towns because that was where the soldiers spent their money. They made sure they catered to all the needs of men in uniform, including cheap, quick bail bondsman, and you could see the judge almost twenty-four seven, pay a fine, and be on transport planes from Okinawa to Camp Pendleton, California. We landed twelve hours later in California on a bright and sunny day. We proceeded by truck to the parade field and was given leave right at that spot, which to me was a wonderful idea since like many others I had filled my seabag half with clothing and the other half with some of that good Vietnam grass, which we had gotten accustomed to and could not leave behind. The women and the children came secondary to the marijuana we loved.

From California, I decided to go home and see my mother and father—mostly, Mom. I had new brothers and sisters I had not yet met. Plus, my younger brother who was also in the military was home at the same time. He was one of the first African Americans to finish West Point Military Academy, and I was very proud of him because he himself had overcome a lot of adversity to achieve what he had achieved. Being a lieutenant, I could not wait to salute him.

But knowing I was the cock of the walk, so to speak, and having served in combat and earned some ribbons and medals, I was pretty proud of myself and was happy with myself even in my state of mind. Well, after seeing my father and the expression on his face, my proudness was short-lived, and somehow I felt he was jealous for some reason. I found out he had been in WWI, and at that time, blacks only served as cooks or domestic help. So after a heated exchange and fifteen days into a thirty-day leave, I said my goodbyes and headed to my next duty station—Camp Lejeune, North Carolina.

I arrived at Camp Lejeune on a Saturday. I remember so well because it was kind of a brisk and windy day and was kind of cool for that time of year. The base was like a deserted town, and I already figured out there must be plenty to do and places to go in the surrounding cities. There was usually plenty of happenings in the service towns because that was where the soldiers spent their money. They made sure they catered to all the needs of men in uniform, including cheap, quick bail bondsman, and you could see the judge almost twenty-four seven, pay a fine, and be on your way. Probably something was worked out between the government and the city leaders.

I spent that entire Sunday walking around the base and getting acquainted with the area so I could report for duty that Monday and find out where I would be spending most of my time. Although this was my second time at Camp Lejeune, I never got to see how large it was because we were restricted to the area for new recruits only.

But I soon found out it was a pretty good-sized place. It was a city itself, and I found myself really anxious to see what it and the surrounding places had to offer. With a little less than ten months to go before I would be discharged, I wanted time to hurry up and fly by. Little did I know that it was the beginning of what would shape my civilian life, as we would say, back in the world.

Well, as always, I found myself back in the outfit I had become accustomed to and enjoyed. The infantry was the best place for me because I loved to camp out, and it gave me a chance to reflect on what I wanted to do when I got out. By that time, I had gotten promoted to corporal E3 and was made a squad leader over weapons platoon, which was an officer's position in combat. Since I was already a combat-tested soldier, they thought my experience would be good for the new recruits.

Well now, it was going on about three months into my duty there, and I went on weekend liberty in the closest little town to the base by the name of Jacksonville, North Carolina. It was full of bars and juke joints, and I happened to meet a young lady there who was married. Her husband was in the Navy, and when he was out to sea, I filled in.

Although I enjoyed the sexual aspect of our relationship, deep down inside, she gave me the real reason why I felt the way I did about women, and I was right all along. They were liars and were manipulative, and all they had to give us men falling into their trap was sex. I knew better, and most of my becoming a man was to stay away from married women. The bad thing about it was, she began to make me feel that it was his fault that he had to leave her and live up to his commitment he had with the Navy. I found myself believing her dishonesty and her reasons for her deceitfulness.

All the reasons why I felt the way I did about women began to surface, and back to the past I went, back to the very beginning, back to where it all started. I started staying on the base and giving excuses why I could not go to see her. I remember she would find her way to the base and bring me gifts in order to show she really cared for me. But it only enhanced my hatred of her and gave me a look at what women would do to keep a man in their cradle of wickedness. I remember some of the times when we were together. He would be coming home, and she would be trying to rush me off. I wanted him to catch us so he would stop being deceived. Then I realized that I was not the first she betrayed him with, and he most likely already knew what kind of woman he had.

But nevertheless I wanted more than that. I decided I wanted a woman of my own, so I finally broke away from her and started going to another place for liberty. It was a three-hour drive, and I knew she could not go there (or so I thought). This place was introduced to me by a young man that was in my squad whose father was a pastor. He was raised in the church just as I was, and at least we had that in common. Anyway, this place was called Kinston, North Carolina, and they had a place called Margret's. At that time, it was the place to go. As a matter of fact, it was the only place to go. I found myself enjoying the atmosphere of the dancing. I was still not of drinking age, but as long as you were military, your money was good. Now my friend was from Philadelphia, and one thing I discovered was that the boys from Philly could sing and dance. Now I could sing, but my dancing was something to be desired. I was like a white boy. I had no rhythm. As a matter of fact, my younger sister would teases me about that (even today). I don't know whether it was my insecurity as a person or what, but I had never been to many places where people danced except in church, and that was what was called a holy dance or shouting, no fancy footwork.

On one particular night, we were hanging out, and I spotted this one special girl. I say special because she had a pretty smile and green eyes that got my attention, and I had to know who she was. And it so happened that my buddy was dating her best friend, and I had gotten to know her. She seemed to be a very likable person, and you know what they say about birds of a feather flocking together, so to me she was absolutely fine. I knew she was the one; plus, all the other guys seemed to want to know her besides those that had already been with her. But that was not my concern. She was in my radar, and I wanted her for more than just a friend. And not to brag but my buddy and I were in the midst of being the most handsome guys in the place. A lot of girls liked me, but due to my issues, I was selective and not easy to talk to.

So that night, we ended up together, and that night was the beginning of a new chapter in my life. I don't know why God led me down the path he took me, but it was one of the most heart-stopping moments of my life. It would change everything that I thought I knew about myself. As I said before, this book is not about blaming anyone or name-dropping. It is about the effect that sexual abuse and other abuses toward a boy child will do and the choices he will make during his growth into manhood. This is not a book to judge or form opinions about. It is a book to help those that are interested in helping cure the effects of abuse and neglect that our children may endure at the very impressionable ages of their lives.

We took a cab to her house, which she was renting, and she explained her situation, that she was living alone and had no one to help her in her current situation. I replied to her that I understood, not knowing what was about to take place in the blink of an eye. As she unlocked the door and we stepped inside, I noticed there were no lights, and then I felt the cold. It was actually colder in the house than it was outside, but none of that would compare to what I would dis-cover next. There were no furniture and no bed to sleep in. Over in the corner, I saw a dresser with the drawers pulled out, and sleeping in the drawers were two babies. The thing that really shook me was the fact that she had left them there by themselves while she went out to the club. In my heart, I began to cry. She saw the look on my face, and she began to cry. It was one thing abuse had done to me, and that was to feel it was my responsibility to protect children no matter whose they were. What I saw made me hurt inside that no one cared about the well-being of those children.

Even after all that I had been through, I had never witnessed anything of this magnitude, because I had never been in the cold and been left alone at least at night and not without a place to sleep. I was torn between anger and hurt. I began to feel a rage building in my soul like I had never had before. Then I saw the look on her face and began to question her about why she had no help, not from family or any of the other guys she had been with, and she explained that her mother was taking care of another child that had a disability and needed constant care.

Believe me, I wanted to run. I knew to run because it's one thing about being abuse as a child (and I can only speak about my own experience), it makes you think you have to protect every child you come in contact with who seems to have no one else to care for them. That was one of the most telling signs, and it's not a good sign. As you read further, you will discover that kindness will become a burden you can't get rid of, and it will use a lot of your energy as you take care of the mess others have created and your time as you try to fix problems you can never fix.

Nevertheless, I stayed there with her, slept on the floor until Monday, and went and had the electricity turned on so there would be heat before I left. Needless to say, I lost my need for a sexual encounter with her. One reason was, it was too cold to take my clothes off. Also I knew I was in trouble because I was supposed to be back on base by 8:00 a.m. Monday morning, even though I did call. But in the military, because you were property of the government, you get to your duty station first, and then if you have to leave, you put your request in. It's not like a job where you can call in late. So when I did return, I had to go before the captain, and my punishment was no leaving the base for two weeks. I received a lecture on what it was like in these service towns and how women took advantage of servicemen. In a way, I was glad that I was given that punishment because I did not want to experience that kind of scene again, I was content in staying on the base and had no reason to go back to Kinston again since I didn't really care for her anyway (or so I thought). Plus, I knew that with my issues, I'd give in because of the children. That was a heavy burden to bear, and I knew that was a weakness I could not shake off. Even in Vietnam, I was always giving to the children. That lonely feeling of not being protected was lodged within me, so deep it was actually a pain deep in my heart. And even though I could forget the mother, I could not forget those two babies alone in the cold.

Anyway, just as I thought I had gotten over that trauma, I encountered here again. It was on my second week of being on the base, and I was relaxing and listening to some good music when I got a call that someone was at the gate, inquiring about me. I thought it might be the lady that was married to the Navy guy, and although I knew there was no place to be alone with her, I would at least have someone to talk to and get a chance to at least look at a woman. But to my surprise, it was that girl from Kinston. She had gotten a ride down with her friends and said she wanted to thank me for what I had done. At first, I didn't want to be bothered and was kind of dry with my conversation, and after having the conversation with my captain, I thought maybe she wanted money, which really was not going to happen. But to my surprise, after I inquired about the children, she said her sister was looking after them. She then put a wad of money in my hand, again thanking me for having the heat turned on. I thought to myself, *That's a first.* I had never had anyone give anything to me, especially after I had given them something. Now I was really confused. Was she really different, or was this a trick?

To make a long story short, we began to see each other on a regular basis. I met her family, and we ended up getting married about three months later. To my surprise, I really started to love her. I filled out the necessary papers for her and the children to get medical care, and things started to look up. The thing about getting married was, my buddy and his girl were married on the same day, which made it more special. And having about four months to go before my discharge, it seemed like perfect timing. Then another bump in the road came up. I had orders to be transferred to Quantico, Virginia, to train officers on how to use the M-60 machine gun or to go back to California and maybe return to Vietnam—that was a difference. No! Not with four months to go. So off to Virginia I went. My wife had a cousin in Norfolk, Virginia, so she followed me there. After a while, she came to live on the base, and again everything was looking up. We also found out we were having another baby, and it was a boy. She was about two months pregnant; to me, that was great.

During this time, I borrowed a friend's car and took that two-hour drive to pick her and the twins up. (I think, it might have been three.) Anyway, I managed to get housing on the base, and for a while, I was good—getting ready to get out of the Marines and having a son coming into the world, plus seeing the twins, who were small for their age, starting to walk. It was a joyous time, and it seemed to keep my mind off my past. Then one day I came home early and saw my wife in a conversation with a guy that lived up the street. I knew him because we met him and his wife while we were shopping at the base commissary, and I could tell by her demeanor that they were having problems. I could see why, as when I approached them, he had a grin like a possum eating you know what. I was not smiling at all—to let him know she was off-limits. Plus, he was not a particularly handsome guy, so I could see his fascination in her, but I wanted him to know that I was not one to play with. I was not a very friendly person. When came to having men friends, I had none!

After I scolded my wife about the dangers of holding conversations with strange men, she realized I had trust issues, which I did admit to. But I never told her why, nor did I want to talk about it. I knew she was pregnant and having an affair was the last thing she had in mind, but I found out later in our marriage that my mistrust was warranted. You will learn as you continue to read that my hatred for women sprang up in a conflicting and drastic way. And while we are on the subject of mistrust, you will find that a person that has been abused and molested will always be attracted to someone that can't be trusted. Somehow they seem to be able to slither their way into your life to add on to the baggage you're already carrying around.

But again this was supposed to be a joyous time in my life, and I decided I was not going to let my issues get in the way of our happiness. I went to the nightclub on the base and had a few drinks and a smoke, of course, and when I got tipsy enough, I proceeded home to get ready for the next day, which would started at 6:00 p.m.

Now here at Quantico, it was a lot different than any other place I had been in while I was in the Marines because it was primary officers that lived there. It was the place they were trained, and their training consisted of a more technical nature than that of an enlisted soldier. Although I was teaching them, they were quick to remind me of my lower rank. My day consisted of saluting nonstop, and if somehow you passed by an officer and did not greet him or by mistake, you not seeing him or her was no excuse. You got your butt chewed out, which was not good for me, because one of my main issues (if you remember) was having no tolerance for authority. Although I would not have a verbal response, my expressions would say it all. And in the end, it got me busted down from an E3 to a private first class, which meant a drop in pay.

But thank God the months went past, and I was discharged. My family and I headed home to Indiana. My wife was about seven months by that time and was almost ready to drop, and here I was, coming back to my father's house with two baby girls that were not biologically mine and a pregnant wife. It was a place that was about as eventful as a chicken in the middle of a pack of turtle doves. You are pecking and scratching, and they just sit and look.

I remember the day well. I got out of the cab from the bus station and knocked on the door, and my father came to the door—no smile, no "Welcome home." (I guess it wasn't my home.) He just had a look of "What the hell do you want?" So right then, I knew my first priority was a job and a place to stay.

Needless to say, by me being a veteran, I seemed to be able to get a job and a place to live in, but this is the real kicker. The place we moved into was the same place I was molested by the babysitter. There were new apartments, but there were in the same area. My front door was exactly where the backyard used to be. And the funny thing was, I did not pay it any attention until years later. That was where my troubles began, and without me realizing it, my issues would confront me head on.

What is going to take place in this segment of the book will be graphic and may make some angry, but please don't judge me. Remember, this is about what happens when a person is sick with anger, mistrust, hatred, PTSD, and other issues and can find no help, not even from the VA. At that time, we had a lot of primary benefits as far as being the first to be hired if there were any jobs, and even that had controversies because some did not think a Vietnam veteran deserved a job at all. Housing was provided in the public housing areas but not a place to go that provided mental help, especially for me, because I had issues before I went to Vietnam. So you know I was jacked up after I got out.

I could never figure out why I had so many issues to deal with all at once— the insecurities, the pent-up hatred, and the mistrust I carried. The most painful one of all was, I was not capable of loving anything or anyone other than animals. I trusted my dog before I trusted a human being, and at that time, it never seemed odd to me. I would always blame my feelings on others, not being able to understand who I was.

It seemed my life stayed full of conflict, and I had no idea where it was coming from. Every little thing seemed to anger me. It didn't make a difference how big or how small. My level of anger was always the same, as if the reason for the problem was to hurt me, as if it was there to take advantage of me or to make me look bad.

But as you will be able to gather from my story, this was just the beginning, one issue after another taking its toll on my life, and I could never get a handle on where it was all coming from, where it began, how joy and happiness always seemed to be just a glance or a fast-moving part of my life experience. When I tried to grab on to the goodness and do the right thing, it never manifested.

I even turned to going to church again, because I was taught that it was the place I could get answers to all my problems, that there was nothing that we suffered that God could not deliver us from. Through it all, my faith (however little) in Him was not going to ever waver. He was somehow the only one I could trust. I also went back to singing with the same spiritual group I started with before I enlisted in the military, and right by my side was my best friend, who seemed to want to follow me in everything I did and also played a great part in me not just giving up on life.

But my first real big disaster came on a Sunday after church. The group had a singing engagement at another church that I attended. My spirit was really high, and I felt really good about myself and thought in my mind that this was the right decision I had made, that somehow God would turn this pent-up evil spirit that had infested my life to a thing of the past. But what was to come next changed everything I thought about church into a mystical bunch of lies, especially since everybody I knew that went was not living right anyway, including my father, who everybody thought was an example of a Christian, well respected everywhere but in his own home.

My mother, who also was raised in the church, only went if there was a special occasion and when the women were doing something that needed her cooking skills in the kitchen, because no one could burn like my mama. But she could tell you all the details of what was going on with all those good Christian folks. She had very little tolerance for most of them and their fake lives.

Back to my disaster. Anyway, that same Sunday, I got home after being gone all day—serving the Lord, mind you. My wife was very angry. She was doing the laundry and was probably angry because I was not there to help, and after I gave it some thought, I realized she was probably right. But I could not see through my issues, and I shut down as if I didn't care. That made her angrier, and she threw the basket at me, which was heavy and full of wet clothes. Somehow she twisted her body and fell, and then I had to take her to the emergency room at the hospital. We were there most of the night, but the doctor gave her a clean bill of health, and we came home, thinking everything was fine. Two days since her fall, she began to complain that the baby was not moving, so I asked her if she should go to the doctor again, and she replied she would be okay since it was almost time to deliver the baby in a few days. So we waited, and little did I know that the next event would change both our lives forever. She went into labor that Friday, and our son was delivered stillborn. That was the day nothing else mattered to me—not church, not her, not even myself. I felt God had taken my son, probably the only thing that would have helped me maintain my sanity. All my issues rose up in me at once.

At first, I thought God had taken him because of what I had suffered as a child and I was not deserving of him. I couldn't quite figure out what had happened. I blamed her for falling. I should have been there to protect him, even though he was not born yet. I failed him, just like my parents failed to protect me. My anger would not let me see past anything else. No one could even show me the sense in this tragedy. No words could even explain it, and I surely didn't want to hear those religious reasons, like it was God's will, or anything of a religious nature. Why would that be God's will? God, who was supposed to love me, how could He hurt me so bad?

I left my wife at the hospital and drove for a while in my car. I don't know how far I went. All I know it was daylight the next morning. I cried every mile

I drove. The only other time I cried was in the Nam, when my fellow Marines were hurt or killed. But this was more pure and intense.

This was the most pain I think I had ever dealt with in my life. Nothing

She was doing the laundry and was probably angry because I was not there to help, and after I gave it some thought, I realized she was probably right. But I could not see through my issues, and I shut down as if I didn't care. That made her angrier, and she threw the basket at me, which was heavy and full of wet clothes. Somehow she twisted her body and fell, and then I had to take her to the emergency room at the hospital. We were there most of the night, but the doctor gave her a clean bill of health, and we came home, thinking everything was fine. Two days since her fall, she began to complain that the baby was not moving, so I asked her if she should go to the doctor again, and she replied she would be okay since it was almost time to deliver the baby in a few days. So we waited, and little did I know that the next event would change both our lives forever. She went into labor that Friday, and our son was delivered stillborn. That was the day nothing else mattered to me—not church, not her, not even myself. I felt God had taken my son, probably the only thing that would have helped me maintain my sanity. All my issues rose up in me at once.

At first, I thought God had taken him because of what I had suffered as a child and I was not deserving of him. I couldn't quite figure out what had happened. I blamed her for falling. I should have been there to protect him, even though he was not born yet. I failed him, just like my parents failed to protect me. My anger would not let me see past anything else. No one could even show me the sense in this tragedy. No words could even explain it, and I surely didn't want to hear those religious reasons, like it was God's will, or anything of a religious nature. Why would that be God's will? God, who was supposed to love me, how could He hurt me so bad?

I left my wife at the hospital and drove for a while in my car. I don't know how far I went. All I know it was daylight the next morning. I cried every mile I drove. The only other time I cried was in the Nam, when my fellow Marines were hurt or killed. But this was more pure and intense. This was the most pain I think I had ever dealt with in my life. Nothing that had ever happened to me was so hurtful and painful—not the sexual abuse by the babysitter, not the verbal abuse by my father, not even the loss of my friends in Vietnam. My firstborn son—and I have been carrying his death around inside all these years. I don't think most of my family even knew about it because after it happened, I shut it up inside. I remember reading about David, about the son God took away from him, and about how he seemed to just move on and accept what God had done. But I could not, because I had not taken anyone's wife. I had done everything in the order He had commanded. I could not figure out what I had done wrong. Why would He punish me in this manner?

In any case, unlike David, who continued to trust and confide in God, I turned away. I put my trust in the only person I knew how to trust—me. I decided I would make my own decisions, not realizing I had been doing that all along and that it was the main reason why things were not working out. Anyhow, I figured it couldn't get any worse.

It's one thing about abuse of any kind; it's like a root. You see the plant on top of the earth, trying to reach its potential but never realizing that the root is the cause of it withering and dying. Abuse hides deep under all your thoughts and your decisions, clouding your judgment and keeping itself secret. If you could tell that everything else would be seen in a different light, you would understand that all your issues stemmed from that one traumatizing event. You have to dig up the root and replant it in good soil so it will grow. Every abuser has been abused, and the only way to stop it is to dig it up and shed some light on it so it will be seen for its real self. That is going to take some real painful doing, which most of us are not ready for, so we become abusers ourselves.

And no one wants to help the abuser. The abuser is thrown away into the trash of life, becoming a monster instead of what he really is—a flawed human being. Besides, my Bible tells me God Himself said He wishes no man to perish, which means there is hope for everyone. Cane killed Abel. Abel was the one that was pleasing to Him. Cane was the one that murdered his brother, and I am sure God could have done away with him, but God allowed him a chance to be redeemed. God would not even allow another human being to touch him. How much more are we to give the abusing person, who most likely has been abused themselves, a chance to seek help?

In spite of everything, I decide just to give up on everything. Nothing was important anymore—not the marriage, not the job, not God, nothing. I just wanted to say, "The hell with life!" Period. I was tired of trying to figure out what was going on that made it so complicated that I could not even have a normal relationship like everyone else. When my intentions were to go right, why did I end up going left? And when I wanted to elevate myself, I ended up going to the basement floor. I knew I wanted to do good, and at that time, I just could not imagine that my attitude and my mental state of mind had been programed from the time I was a child until this very moment, that I had been set on a course of failure. No matter how I tried to stop and get off that ride, it was already ingrained in my DNA, so to speak. It was part of me and who I would become, and there was nothing I could do to stop it.

So I gave up religion and turned my attention to the world. It looked much better out there anyway. It seemed people were enjoying themselves more and cared less about the things that church people deemed important. Nothing mattered but having fun, moving fast, and not thinking of the consequences of your actions. After all, no one seemed to care about the toll it would take on me being molested by a grown woman and about why I acted out in such a way that should have been alarming by any stretch of the imagination, and about why it would go unnoticed by those who were supposed to be my protection—parents, teachers, police, anybody.

So after leaving my wife, I heard of a rock band that was giving tryouts to vocalists and was formed by a couple of older gentlemen in the next town and had some good weekend gigs, which was fine with me since I was working during the week. I guess the good Lord already knew what my life was going to consist of, so it's one thing He did do. He gave me the voice to sing, and that is one thing I could do well. I wish they had *American Idol* back then. I probably would have been famous. In any event, I became a part of the group, and we did mostly college gigs and some clubs. By this time, I had reached drinking age and could get in most places, because believe it or not, there were some places you could not get in unless you were twenty-five. It was due to the younger folks' behavior. But since I was a member of the band, I had no problem, and although I was not a big drinker, I did smoke a little, enough to keep my composure on stage and to perform well.

Things started to look up, and I actually was doing quite well. Besides my paycheck from my job, I was making an extra $600 for a Friday and Saturday gig, and if we played on Thursdays, I would pull in an extra $200. Back in those days, that was money, and I found out a very funny thing—that by union scales, a vocalist got paid more than the musicians. So life was good for this twenty-one-year old black male from small-town Indiana, and I was not missing the church scene at all.

As time went on, we started to do really well, and we became very popular, especially around the college campuses all over Indiana and Illinois, such as Saint Mary's College in Notre Dame, Indiana University–Purdue, and many others. Our managers thought it would be best that we stayed in that circuit rather than what was called the Chitlin Circuit, and the money was better also. So we grew, and people were telling us we should look into trying to record, which didn't sit well with our managers because that meant they would not be home with family. Plus, they owned a local newspaper, and they just weren't ready for that. But we were; we were younger, and the bright lights were in our eyes. On one particular day, a gentleman from Gary, Indiana, checked us out at one of our local gigs and invited us to a talent show in Gary, Indiana, and almost guaranteed we would be a shoo-in to win. The most incredible thing about it was, one of the attractions at the talent show was also the Jackson Five, although we didn't know it at the time. We were all geared up to go, and we were looking forward to the opportunity to show our stuff. But needless to say, since most of the musicians were family-oriented guys, that opportunity fell through. We ended up at Indiana University for their homecoming, and although we rocked the place, most of us that were vocalists were not satisfied. We wanted more, and we felt we were good enough to have more.

We were together for almost three years, and between working and the band, I saved up a pretty good nest egg and had a nice car and was popular as a hometown boy. But I wanted to spread my wings in the music world, so I quit the band and decided to take piano lessons and strike out on my own. And to my surprise, since I was so busy, I did not have a great social life, and sex was not a real big deal. It meant I didn't have to think about the problem of exploiting my sexual habits or appetite and also my profound dislike of dealing with the distaste I had for women.

But later on, you will see how that dislike would play a major part in the type of women I chose to have a relationship with and how it made me more and more sure that they were worse human beings on earth. In the next chapter, you will understand how a young male child's life can be affected by molestation and the trauma it puts them through.

CHAPTER 6

PROMISCUOUS LIFESTYLE

Ladies and gentlemen, in this chapter, there will be some graphic descriptions, and they are not there to increase the intensity of the book but are necessary to interject the reasons people should watch over their children and protect them from sexual predators. Make no mistake about it—it will ruin your child's life, especially for male, because he is not going to tell. He will live a destructive and abusive life, harming not only himself but many others along the way.

As I mentioned before, eventually the band would break up. Just before we decided to disperse, we did one more gig, and it happened to be in a place that also would become a major part of my life and further illustrated that I let my past set the direction in which I was headed. Now the place happened to be not far from where I lived, even though it was in another state. It was a little town just over the Indiana state line, about forty miles, called Benton Harbor. It was in the state of Michigan. Although it was close, I had no idea where it was, and even though Niles, Michigan, was just over the line, people from Indiana would visit there every Sunday because the bars and nightclubs were closed on Sundays in Indiana. Everyone would head to Niles, to a place in the country, and I mean just that—in the country. But it was a good place to party, and sometimes if you did not want to party, you could go get beer and bring it back across the state line to Indiana and party at home. In any case, that was about as far as we would venture into the state of Michigan. Plus we heard bad things about the police and how they would treat you if got caught in their state.

In any case, our manager happened to land a gig at a place called the East End Bar, and it sat right off the highway we would take from Indiana, sort of a straight shot and easy to find if you were driving by yourself, which I did most of the time. Our first performance was to be on a Friday night, which was their talent show night, and we found out they were looking for a house band, which suited our manager fine. That meant good money and a steady place to play, but little did we know that this was the hometown of Sinbad, the great comedian, who also got his start there. When we arrived, the place was packed, and we knew that landing a spot there could really pay off. But we had to compete with other bands, and some had already performed that Thursday before we were considered. Needless to say, we were introduced second, and the band before us was okay. We were a new-style band and played more up-to-date music, and our organ player was one of the most horrific entertainers around. He was blind, and when we led him to the stage, I could see the look on people's faces, wondering what was going on and if he were Stevie Wonder. He could have very well been! He had a special gift and could mimic anybody he wanted to and sound like the person who recorded the original song.

Anyway, we rocked the house that night, and even though we were only supposed to do two songs, we ended up closing things out. The people still did not want to go home, and people were at the bar, trying to convince the owner that we were the band they wanted to hear every night. Needless to say, we signed a six-month contract, and the pay was pretty good. We were offered a percentage of the door, and by the looks of things, this was to our favor. And also this began a new chapter in my life, which would end up making me come face-to-face with my issues again.

The contract we signed had us starting two weeks from the date we signed it, and it gave us a chance to finish the contract with the nightclub in Indiana, and that was where my trouble began, on that Saturday night, while the band was on break. My ex-wife wasn't my ex yet since we had not filed for divorce and I didn't care anyway. I was going to do what I wanted to. No woman was not even worth me going through what it took for me to get rid of her. The more hurt, the better. I happened to be with another woman that night, who didn't know I was married, and I did not even care enough to let her know. One thing about being molested by a woman (speaking for myself) is that it turns you into an introvert, and even though you are afraid to approach most women, you know all the things to do to make them approach you. It makes you feel more secure about the relationship. But the downside is, you are also afraid of telling the truth about your situation, which will lead to some awkward conflicts.

This night, my ex saw me with this other lady and confronted me, and I felt she had no right to because she was the one to blame for everything that went wrong in our marriage and the loss of our son. And my hatred for her—not only her, but all women—came to the surface in a rage. I to this day cannot explain it, but I cursed her to no end, and she slapped me. I guess it was to bring me back to my senses, but it didn't help. I began to assault her, and to this day, I cannot tell you all that I did or did not do.

If you are reading this book, please, this is not a novel about some story I am telling. It is about what molestation and abuse can do to a male child, so we can begin to watch them and never take it for granted that another woman will not take advantage of them when they are out of your sight. I'm putting it all out there so men will began to seek help and we can stop being the monster we are portrayed to be and become kind and loving as we ought to be, as God intended us to be.

When we hear of female schoolteachers taking advantage of young men, we seem to sweep it under the rug, but if it's the other way around, it's big news, because we figure a young man should think of this as a feather in his cap. I remember watching Judge Mathis one time explaining about the trauma caused by the little girls when they used to chase him and throw him down and kiss him. These were girls his own age. If that was trauma, just think of what a grown woman can cause to a male child who has had no experience whatsoever in being touched and is made to do things against his will.

Back to the issue at hand. Anyway, the young lady I was with somehow brought me to my senses and rushed me to the car, and we headed to her house, which was in Michigan. I felt safe once we crossed the state line. Needless to say, when I'm in that state of rage, there is nothing a woman could say or do to make me calm down. I have to be alone, which she was fully in agreement with. But this also would set the course for a three-year relationship that would also end in disaster. Keep reading.

The relationship started out in an unusual fashion, as all my relationships seemed to for some reason. I seemed to be attracted to women that had some type of issue that made them stand out in a crowd, or it could have been me, because I always tried to make myself stand out. I don't know whether it was my low self-esteem that made me act as if I had to dress better and look better than the rest of the men around me, you know class with no class. I wanted people to know and see me. As I was saying, the relationship started during a show at the East End Bar in Benton Harbor, Michigan. I spotted this beautiful black woman standing on a chair, trying to see me perform that night. I just sang a song I had written; it was called "Merry Go Round of Love." I never recorded it, but it seemed to be a big hit and was always requested by someone, especially the women. But I noticed the effort she was putting in to get my attention, which was right up my alley. As I stated earlier in my book, because of my introverted feelings, it made it easier for me to start a conversation with someone if I knew they were interested in me. So during break time—or as we would say in the entertainment business, a pause for the cause—I went over and introduced myself, and we proceeded to the bar for drinks. Anyway, to make a long story short, we ended up sleeping together and started seeing each other. I liked her company, which was all I needed, because in spite of her looks, she had three other children and was somewhat insecure and was always on the edge of drama. On top of that, she ended up getting pregnant, which really added fuel to the fire. She became very jealous and possessive to the point that it interfered with my job and my nightlife, and that I couldn't have.

But what broke the camel's back was when we had a gig in Chicago.

It was a very important one and was a good opportunity to further my state line. Needless to say, when I'm in that state of rage, there is nothing a woman could say or do to make me calm down. I have to be alone, which she was fully in agreement with. But this also would set the course for a three-year relationship that would also end in disaster. Keep reading.

The relationship started out in an unusual fashion, as all my relationships seemed to for some reason. I seemed to be attracted to women that had some type of issue that made them stand out in a crowd, or it could have been me, because I always tried to make myself stand out. I don't know whether it was my low self-esteem that made me act as if I had to dress better and look better than the rest of the men around me, you know class with no class. I wanted people to know and see me. As I was saying, the relationship started during a show at the East End Bar in Benton Harbor, Michigan. I spotted this beautiful black woman standing on a chair, trying to see me perform that night. I just sang a song I had written; it was called Merry Go Round of Love. I never recorded it, but it seemed to be a big hit and was always requested by someone, especially the women. But I noticed the effort she was putting in to get my attention, which was right up my alley. As I stated earlier in my book, because of my introverted feelings, it made it easier for me to start a conversation with someone if I knew they were interested in me. So during break time—or as we would say in the entertainment business, a pause for the cause—I went over and introduced myself, and we proceeded to the bar for drinks. Anyway, to make a long story short, we ended up sleeping together and started seeing each other. I liked her company, which was all I needed, because in spite of her looks, she had three other children and was somewhat insecure and was always on the edge of drama. On top of that, she ended up getting pregnant, which really added fuel to the fire. She became very jealous and possessive to the point that it interfered with my job and my nightlife, and that I couldn't have.

But what broke the camel's back was when we had a gig in Chicago. It was a very important one and was a good opportunity to further my singing career, and I needed that to come out of the factory. In any case, against her ramping and raving, I went to Chicago for that weekend and returned only to find her in a worse condition than she was when I left. She began to accuse me of seeing other women, which was far from the truth, because I was afraid of cheating on anyone I was in a relationship with, which was contrary to what everyone thought and what I portrayed myself as—which was a flamboyant playboy. Let me explain. Because of my lack of self-confidence and always trying to hide my little secret of sexual abuse, the attention was all I wanted. Being a playboy was the image I had to portray for the men around me. They were players. They loved women, whereas in my case I hated them in secret. One was all I needed just to not be alone and just to have someone to spend time with and quench my sexual urge on. Of course, she didn't know this since I displayed no emotions or any type of love except when we were making love. I displayed more attention to the fact that she was carrying my child than to her as my partner.

But on this particular Sunday, I came to her apartment, which was home at the time since I had moved in with her, expecting to chill and rest up for work the next day, plus the thirty-mile ride to Indiana. But it was not to be so. We argued for more than five hours to the point that I had to get out of the house. As I turned and started down the stairs, she jumped onto my back, and I felt something sharp rip through my clothing. I could feel the sting of the object on my skin. I thank God for the self-defense classes I took in the Marines and it being winter time in Michigan. I turned, and as she swung for my face, I grabbed her arm and somehow took the object from her, which turned out to be a box opener—you know, the kind with the razor attached to it. Nevertheless, a rage came up in me, partly from being in combat and partly from my hatred of whom she represented, and that was a woman whom I had no love for or trust in, in spite of our relationship. I put the razor to her throat, and in my mind, I wanted to slice her throat.

Now, readers, please pay very close attention to what I'm about to share with you. This is very important. Even though I was in a moment of rage and anger and about to end her life, which would have been very easy to do, I looked down on her stomach and saw my child that she was carrying. Although I had no love for her, I felt the need for my child to be protected. I want to emphasize, as I have so often mentioned in this book, that my most important cause before anything was something I felt I never had, and that was protection. I knew that if I killed her, my child would die. Also because she was only about four months along, that feeling of wanting to give protection to my child seemed to take priority over that feeling of hatred and anger for her. Plus I had already lost my firstborn son, and also my second born because of his mother's lies of infidelity to her husband. What took place next may astonish you. I took the box opener and threw it on the floor and escorted her back up the apartment stairs and consoled her because she was frantic about what had just happened. After things cooled down a bit, I went to the hospital to the emergency room, and to my surprise, I saw that she had cut through my winter coat (a wool tweed overcoat), my herringbone suit, all the way to my skin. The cut was so thin I only needed butterfly stitches. Thank God for winter in Michigan. The doctor also informed me that one centimeter to the left and she would have hit my spine, however close that was. I still carry that reminder to this day. After being released from the hospital, I thought it best if I were to go elsewhere, so I gathered my few belongings, and off I went.

Eventually, our contract with the place we were at ended, and like I said before, most of the band members had families and ended up going about their regular routine of working and taking care of their families. Some had been employed for five and ten years and was not about to quit their jobs. But me, although I had been on my job for a while myself, I wanted to continue my singing career, and if you were a good vocalist, you could always find a band needing a good singer. At that time, I was more than good. I eventually quit my job and went on the road full-time with another band. We were playing two and three nightclubs a night, and the money was better than it was working five and six days a week. I had my own apartment, car, clothes, diamonds, and money. Life was good. Even though it was not Hollywood, it felt like it. I was on my way.

The problem was, even though things were looking good, the women stopped looking at me as the playboy that I had pretended to be. They labeled me as a tease because I would only go so far. They did not know that my issue of sexual molestation stopped me from wanting a real relationship. It was almost like having an erectile dysfunction. I was just not interested in having sex because of my incompetence in having feelings of loving anyone, and deep inside, I felt nothing but contempt for a woman.

This is what I really want those that read this book to understand how sexual abuse robs a man of having a normal relationship throughout his life. It puts a burden on him to perform sexually because of what he has been exposed to as a baby boy, not even knowing what an erection was for and forced to do things he had no understanding about, except making another person feel good.

So the ladies soon caught on and kept their distance from me. Some wondered whether I was gay or not, and the ones that I had relationships with thought I was just a good man because I didn't cheat and they had all that good sex to themselves, not knowing that pleasing them was no indication of me being in love.

As you will soon see in your reading of this book, not protecting your child, male or female, will have catastrophic consequences and will cause great emotional damage throughout their whole life as a child and adult, and they may never recover.

Let's move on. I started singing with another band, and what I enjoyed about this band was, they had women vocalists. One of them even played the bass guitar, and that was to me an amazing thing. I loved to share the stage with her because a lot of women were intimidated by her. This kept the wolves off me, so to speak, and at the end of the show, I could leave in peace and didn't have to explain myself to anyone my lack of attention to them.

As time went on, I managed to stay with the band about two years, and we were planning on doing a recording and going big time. For once, I was with a band where everybody was on board, and we were like family. That was a real draw to me, and I was ready to pursue my dream. But again, as fate would have it, this time in my life would end in the most dramatic fashion that ended all I've ever dreamed about.

I remember this day as if it were yesterday. I was at the top of my game. I was free, single, and disengaged. I was happy. What most people can't understand about abuse of any kind is that being alone is the cure to the secret. You don't have to explain your secret because there is nobody there to explain it to. You don't have to work around, trying to hide it, if you say or do something that will cause you to create a rift in the relationship and the other person does not understand what they have done to cause the action taken by you. Most of the time, they have done nothing; it is simply because of the bruises and pain of your past—no trust, no appreciation, and mostly, no love. Yes, there is affection to a certain degree and what I call a surface emotion but nothing as deep as love. And the funny thing is, some live their whole lives this way. Some are able to hide, while some are not. It shows in their treatment of the other person who is supposed to be the closest to them.

Anyway, on this particular day—or should I say night—I was sent to pick up a young man who was to replace the drummer, who quit for some reason. I never knew why to this day, nor did I inquire about the reason. All I knew was that his name was Joe, and I was elected by my manager to go pick him up and bring him to the location we were booked at that night, which was on a Friday. The starting time was 10:00 p.m., so I left the set at about 7:30 p.m. so I could make the forty-minute trip and be back on time.

So mission accomplished, and on the way to the event, he decided he needed some cigarettes. I did not smoke at that time; although I smoked briefly in the military, I had given them up a couple of years ago. But I let him out to get the smokes, and it was just beginning to get dark. I could see that the store owner was preparing to close, but he went in anyway. As I sat in the car for a few minutes, probably about three minutes, I happened to see that this Joe person had a gun in the store owner's face, along with his wife. Yes, panic came over me, because even in my condition, robbing someone was never in my thoughts or even considered. I had no idea what or why this was happening. In any event, I drove off because I would have no part of that! He was on his own as far as I was concerned.

As I was speeding down the street, I could see him in my rearview mirror, running frantically behind me. Like a fool, I pulled over and picked him up, and I began to cuss him to no end. He offered me money, but I refused and dropped him off and proceeded to the house of my babies' momma and began to explain what had happened and asked for advice on what must I do. Should I go to the police or not? Her answer was no. Because I had already implicated myself, so I stayed the night at her house and had no sleep.

Now this is the most unusual part of this story. The next morning, I had made up in my mind that this was a secret I could not carry. I was already carrying enough for someone else. I was not going to carry this shame for him. So I called the police and told them what had happened, and I was coming down to turn myself in and give a statement and put my trust in the law. Wrong! Anyway, I went down as I promised, and as soon as I walked in, they acted like I had pulled the robbery myself. Even after I gave my statement, I found out that their intended goal was to send another black boy to prison. Honesty be dammed. Truth had no bearing on the case.

But even in my sorrow, God had a plan. My bond was set, and to my surprise, guess who came to get me out. My father. That was the first time he had ever exhibited any kind of emotion on my behalf. Even though I had moved out and was on my own, he came, and more importantly, he did not show any kind of anger or shame as to why I was there.

That was the first time I really thought he honestly loved me as a son. I found out later it was the persistence of my mother that got him to come and see me, but thank God he did come.

So now, I was out of jail on bond, but being out on bond to me was like being a slave with a long chain. You were only allowed to go so far before you were yanked back into reality. Anyway, I went back to work, and since I worked in Indiana, no one seemed to know about my dilemma. I didn't know my court date, and I kept hoping that somehow the law would find out that I had nothing to do with the robbery, that in fact I left the real crook in the dust, even though I didn't turn him in. Snitching was a code of honor, but lying was another name for it, as I soon found out.

It took almost a year for them to finally set a court date, and although the prosecutor in Michigan allowed me to stay in Indiana while awaiting trail, I had to return to Michigan. Nevertheless, I still had faith that I would be vindicated, especially since I had turned myself in. How much more honest could you get than that?

So I went to trial, facing thirty to sixty years for armed robbery, and in Michigan, if you were a participant in any way, you faced the same charges as the person that actually committed the crime. But like I said, they somehow had figured it out that I took no part in the crime. Wrong again. They were nice enough to break my charge down to a class D misdemeanor, which was a five-year maximum. Well, lucky me, I got two and a half to five. It took my breath away, but it wasn't until I actually got to prison that I saw what God was doing. It was while I was out on bond that I had committed the real crimes, and they were crimes of hatred. I had assaulted my then girlfriend, and she called the police and then dropped the charges, though it was still on record. And I had stopped working and was hanging out with all the street gangs. In other words, I was becoming a real gangster and had one foot in prison and one foot in the cemetery, and I began to realize God was saving my life.

After I got to prison and was checked in, I was told I would not go behind the walls but would be sent to one of the farm programs, which was for those who were there for crimes such as mine. Again in my mind, I was there for nothing, but in reality, God had me there for something. While I was there, I began to see that I could have been like the guy that committed the robbery. He was never getting out. He broke his parole and robbed people and committed other crimes that I didn't know about. I was glad because he had exposed me to a life-shaking experience, and I wanted to see him suffer for all he had done.

After a while, I began to settle in on the farm and actually began to enjoy it. Work was hard, but thank God I was no stranger to hard work and that I liked being around the animals. We pulled potatoes out of the ground in the hot sun, but in Michigan, the sun was not out long before it was time to end the day. But as I began to see what was going on in my life, I started to read the Word (the Bible) and began to read about Joseph and how God put him in charge of things even while he was serving time for a crime he didn't commit, and as I began to pray, I began to see things beginning to change. Now I did go to the hole once, but even then, God was still working. I remember one hot day we were in the field, digging up potatoes, and all the black guys happened to notice that all the white guys were sitting in the shade while we were still working. We began to murmur and complain. Then I, with my bold self, asked the guard what was going on, why all the white prisoners were sitting in the shade and the black prisoners were still working. It seemed like slavery to me. Then he replied, "No, it's not slavery because even they did not work hard enough." Then he said he should have been a slave master; he would have worked them twice as hard. And in his voice was great authority. He said that if I did not get back to work, I would be placed in the hole. Then again that anger that I had carried all through my childhood and through my time with the Marine Corps reared up in me, and I bluntly told him take me to the hole, that I was done being his slave.

So he called the guards to come pick me up, and me and my big mouth got me five days in the hole. Now mind you, this was in Jackson, Michigan—the prison with the highest wall in the country—and I was put in the hole for five days. But as I began to pray, God began to work. After the third day, they came to get me for me to go see the warden, who I found out was also African American, and he began to explain to me that I could get out of the hole that day if I promised to follow the prison rules and submit to this man's authority. Then he asked me why I volunteered to go to the hole. I explained to him my reasoning and let him know that I realized why I was there and would never volunteer to go to the hole for something stupid. I would go again for what he said. He then told me to wait until he investigated my allegations. I guess he must have found out that I was telling the truth because later that day, I was let out and returned to the farm and was welcomed by all the other inmates. A month later, I was put in charge of housekeeping, which meant I ran the barracks and did not have to go out in the sun to pick potatoes again.

For the first time, God really showed me who I was. In prison, he showed me I was somebody in spite of all the anger and bitterness and hatred I was carrying inside. I was respected by all my peers, and even though some of them were guilty of their crimes, including murder, they all respected me, even the Muslim brothers. And the most inspirational thing was, when I was paroled after serving eighteen months, they said to me, "You don't belong here. We do." I prayed for them and told them they didn't belong there either and to seek the one that helped me get through the prison bars, never to return. That was over fifty years ago.

You know, they say time heals all wounds. Well, it may have put a Band-Aid on them, but healed I wasn't. As a matter of fact, I found myself with a more selfish and non-caring attitude than I had before I went to prison. No one cared for me, so why should I be concerned about anyone but me? After all, I did my time with no one's help, at least no one but my babies' mama. And she got pregnant and had another child while I was locked up, so I definitely scratched her off my list. I was ready to move on with my life. Although she tried to get with me, I felt that inner rage that made me feel disgust and malice like I had been molested again.

I guess somehow God understood me better than I understood myself, because He continued to bless me even in my state of madness and hatred. He opened doors that I might not otherwise have been able to open on my own. I knew it had to be God, but I refused to completely give my life to Him. I wanted to do my own thing, yet He was always there.

Since I was on parole for nine months, I had to find a job while staying at the halfway house, and it seemed immediately I found employment—and not just any job, but a job that paid well. That should have made me humble and grateful, but instead it made me more selfish and more determined to prove I was a step above everyone else, that there was no one better than me, that even though no one ever protected me and no one ever covered for me, I still was going to be top dog.

Now there was one good thing I did do. While I was incarcerated for those eighteen months, I enrolled in a correspondence course in accounting. I wanted to learn how to manage and save money and use it to my advantage, because I remember the trouble my mother had in trying to get my father to save and manage his money. It seemed he was always borrowing from others even though he made a good living. I did not want that to be me. I wanted to be the lender, not the borrower. He was happy shopping at Goodwill, and I like the best. Especially when it came to clothing, I wanted mine to be new. Looking good on the outside hid the dirt of how I felt on the inside, the filthiness I endured as a child, which no one could ever understand.

Now before we go on, let me give you an overview of my life so far. I was sexually molested from the age of four until five or six, physically and mentally abused by my father, enlisted in the Marines at fifteen, was deployed in Vietnam at seventeen, honorable discharged at twenty, married and divorced, became a vocalist in a band at twenty to twenty-three, also worked a job, lost my first child, went to prison and got out, and found out my last name wasn't really my last name (and still hadn't turned twenty-five). Plus, I've endured racism along the way, not counting some things I may have forgotten. Don't forget, I am writing this book from memory at the ripe old age of seventy-two.

For the sake of not repeating myself, I returned to what we call civilization and began my life over, or should I say I began a new chapter. I was determined not to repeat my mistakes of the past. The first few months of getting out were hectic. I stayed in the halfway house and did not have too much freedom, except when I had to work and the few hours I had before returning to the halfway house. I remember one day I ran into a lady friend and took her up on her invitation to come to her apartment for dinner, which was great because my daily meals were fast food and a home-cooked meal was too good to pass up (plus the other expectations I had). Well, I ended up oversleeping and got back to the halfway house a few hours late. I tried to sneak in but got caught in the act, and the officer in charge that night read me the riot act and confirmed that I had broken my parole, so back to prison I would go. The very next morning, I had packed my things to return to prison. Then my parole officer came in, and he also read me the riot act. I was truthful about where I had been and had to give him all the details. Now remember, although the charge I had was reduced to a misdemeanor, the crime was committed at night, so they wanted to make sure that I had not been out, robbing someone. I hope some young man reading this book will pay attention and remember that if you are caught with the snakes, you are considered a snake. So after confirming that I was where I said I was, he let me know that that would be my first and only warning. That was all I needed.

Anyway after about nine months, I was about to finish my stay there, and I met a young man that had heard about my singing and said he was in a vocal group and they needed another guy to fill in. At first, I said no because I was working and had saved a little money and was not really interested in entertainment, because that was what got me into trouble in the first place. Besides, the manager of the group had just gotten out of prison himself, for pandering, and I knew that was a no-go. After about a week, when I was so sure I had made the right decision, he got in touch with me again and explained that while he had been in prison, he had met some guys that had connections and he had written some songs he wanted to record. He also assured me that everything was on the up and up, so I decided I was not going to commit until I talked to my parole officer, because even though I was getting out of the halfway house, I had a year of parole left to do.

But to my surprise, he gave me his blessing and told me to just make sure I reported when it was scheduled, and I made a solemn promise that I would. Not only that, but after we did our first show, I happened to see him in the audience. I knew he was checking on me, but at the same time, I was glad he took the time to come. After the show, he gave me a thumbs up before he left, and that was really special. I was so grateful he let me pursue my dream when he could have easily said no. It was at that time when I felt God had something special for me after all I had been through, and I began to feel as if I was on my way to greatness.

Now the other four guys that formed the group had all grown up together and, at first, did not seem to be in any hurry to welcome an outsider into their close-knit family, especially one that had just come out of prison. Even though it was for just a short while and even though I was a very talented singer, I didn't belong in their little circle, so I would have to earn my badge of honor, and it wasn't going to be easy. Also even though the person who put the group together had just been released from prison, he had a connection to them that I didn't have, and that was the fact that he was born and raised in the same hometown as them and they knew one another's families.

But after months and months of rehearsing routines and blending our voices, I slowly began to earn their respect, and they began to notice that even though I had been to prison and they were always able to come and go as they pleased, I surpassed them in my ability to blend in with all the so-called players of that day. Everybody seemed to recognize me when I appeared, and they did not understand why.

And what they really couldn't understand was why I avoided the social activities; why when I was invited to their functions at their homes, I would only come every now and then; and why I avoided familiarity. Their women seemed to notice that I had advanced beyond their men's abilities to live up to the standards that they pictured in their minds when they first met them. After all, they had a job, and their men did not want to work, even though some of them had children. Each day was a party, and when I was around, they seemed to point that out to their men.

The only one that came close was married and worked and, like me, was hoping one day that would come to an end and we all would be rich. Nevertheless, I managed to kind of keep my distance and also have a good relationship with everyone, and we began to gain popularity as a singing group. Everyone knew we would be recording soon, and the city anticipated our first release of many.

But before I get to that, let me back up and explain some things that will help you, the reader, better understand my motives for doing the things I did and living in such a way that seemed I was antisocial. First of all, the secret of being sexually depressed was that main reason. Again being sexually molested is almost like having ED. The only difference is that you can get the erection but have no desire to use it, which to me is even worse. So many a night, when all my friends thought I was laid up with some lady friend, I was home alone, wishing I could fall in love and have a normal relationship. And the funniest thing of all was, it even took the desire to masturbate from me. Sometimes I would just lie there and cry, because there were many fine ladies I could have been with but I had no desire for. No, I wasn't gay. That was the furthest thing from my mind. Sex seemed to me unpleasurable, and if I did choose someone to be with, the relationship would be destroyed in a matter of weeks. I was a wonderful lover but had no desire to keep trying to please someone I hated in secret and had no feelings for.

The point I am trying to make is, if I stayed any longer, I would become abusive to that person because I could never see the good in them. I could never see past the idea that the reason I was there was to perform and let myself be consumed by their lust and desires, and even if it wasn't true, I could never get past my own reasoning.

And as you continue to read this story, you will began to understand why that one act of abuse would take me down the path I would go and why it is so important for fathers and mothers to keep up with their male child. One act of lust from an uncaring woman or man who is only thinking of themselves can ruin your son or daughter for the rest of his or her life. They may never recover. They will either be killed or spend the rest of their life in prison, especially the male.

As this story continues to unfold, you will become aware of the fact that as I got older, it became harder to have a normal relationship without the fear of re-visiting all the episodes that took place in the closet. I expected every woman to perform all the sexual acts that I desired and to let me perform what I deemed satisfying to her, and most of the time, I was involved in one-night stands because of the disappointment of being impatient.

Now back to my story. As time went on, I was introduced to one of the group members' sister. A cutie she was, but as we became closer, the fear of her lack of experience began to show. You see, being sexually abused gives you an insight on what to look for in a woman or in her conversation that will let you know if she can be the one to satisfy the lustful appetite you've developed from childhood. I guess the one good thing that came out of my situation is, I did not like young girls. I did not develop the desire for women younger than thirty. As a matter of fact, the older, the better. By then they have usually fully developed, with nice butts and big breasts. That's what I could remember about my abuser, and I don't know if the reason was that I was so small that even if she didn't have fully developed breasts or behind, they seemed big to me. Of course, as I got older and the women became younger, my limit was still at least twenty-five, but my woman of choice was forty or forty-five.

But anyway we stopped seeing each other, and she ended up getting married and was still married when I last saw her (maybe she's still married to this day). Just think of how I could have ruined her life if I had proceeded with the relationship. Most abusers know how to start a relationship, but it is in the relationship where the problem starts. And while I preferred a woman of intelligence and had a good job, I always ended up with nasty street women because there was no limit to their sexual abilities. As you can see, I have become damaged goods, and that would remain with me until I was well into my sixties. Not only that, but it I began to change my lifestyle. I became a street lover myself. It seemed more exciting to me, and it fulfilled my needs without all the hassle, even though there was always much drama.

Now as far as my singing career went, it began to flourish. We recorded a forty-five; it was on the radio and every juke box on the Chitlin Circuit, and we were doing shows with some of the popular groups, such as the Manhattans and the Dells. So we were on the road to success even though we were not getting paid much, which seemed to be a disappointment. But our popularity was growing, and the women were plentiful.

By the way, the name of the group was the End Results, and the song was "Reminiscing." It was also featured on one of the Dells' last album in 1975. You can still find it on YouTube. I think it never got past the top forty. Oh, well. A funny thing is, I would begin to measure my life by the results of that recording. Maybe I will always be in the midrange of success. It reminded me of the scripture Matthew 13:8, which talks about sowing seeds on good ground; some brought forth a hundredfold and some sixtyfold and some thirtyfold. I was always above thirtyfold but never reached sixtyfold, and a hundredfold was out of reach for me. It wasn't until later in life that I began to accept that that was where God wanted me to be in my life. So I was satisfied in the fortyfold because that was my measure of life. Even though I fell below the forty sometimes, it was easy for me to climb back up to forty, but it seemed God knew how I would act if I reached that hundredfold. (Does that make sense?) It taught me my success is where God wants me, which is where I can do the most good. But as you're going to see as you read further, goodness is always mixed with failure and disaster, and it lets us know that as in the life of Jesus, goodness has its price.

CHAPTER 7

SALVATION BRINGS LIFE!

I guess being raised in the church was probably the most important part of my life because if there's one thing I know, it's that if things seem to go so wrong that it seems like there is no way out, I was taught to get on my knees and pray even if it was after I had tried a thousand times to solve the problem or problems myself. Anyway, I started attending church. Although I was not a member of any certain denomination or religion, I felt some kind of spiritual connection with the Creator, and that seemed to help me feel good about myself and lift some of the burden of self-pity I felt inside.

At this time in my life, things seemed to be taking a turn for the better. It was somewhere in the late seventies or early eighties. I had a fairly good-paying job and was driving a little Chevy Nova. It was not really my type of car, but I had paid cash for it. It was on its second year under my ownership, and to me, that was perfect. I was dating, but there was nothing serious. I liked it that way, and it allowed me to discover that that there were some women that just wanted to be dated—you know, go to dinner or a movie, have sex sometimes or just a kiss at other times. But these are the women I began to really like because they had begun to change the perspective I had perceived of all women. Most were good, honest, hardworking women, although I had an instance where one had put something in my drink to steal a piece of jewelry I was wearing and I ended up passing out in my car outside the bar. Somehow I just blamed her and didn't hold it against all of them at all. That let me know that I was making some kind of progress in my situation. Anyway, this young lady ended up going to prison because she pulled the same trick on another guy who happened to be an undercover policeman, and I summed it up as a lesson on both her behalf and mine.

As I so humbly stated earlier, I was raised in the church, and although God had brought me through a lot of things in my life and my father was a devout Christian, I don't think that up until this point, I really knew God or Jesus Christ, for that matter. But I always believed it was Him that was always showing up at the right time to rescue me from my own hatred of myself and those I came in contact with. I somehow recall this time in my life as being very vibrant and full. I had a good job and a little Chevy Nova. Although it wasn't my preferred type of car, I was content because it was always reliable and was in fairly good shape.

And at this time in my life, I think I was about thirty-one or maybe thirty-two. I realized that something was missing in my life, and although I was dating, I kind of wanted a close relationship with someone. One sunny day after work, I went to my apartment, cleaned up, and decided to ride through the neighborhood, which was only block over from where I had moved to in South Bend, Indiana, from Elkhart, Indiana, to be close to my job. Besides, I had lived in Elkhart all my life, and this gave me a chance to meet new people. I also had relatives through my father's first wife that lived there. But on this particular day, as I was riding, I spotted this beautiful tall dark young lady standing on the sidewalk. She had smooth skin and a shape like (as we said in those days) a brick house. It must have been in the month of July or August, which were the two hottest months in Indiana, but I broke out like James Brown in a cold sweat. As I got closer to where she was standing, the more I felt like she was the one, but also the closer I got to her, the more the fear of not being good enough began to rise in my bones.

People, this is very important—what I'm about to explain. Please remember this is coming from a man that is almost seventy-three years old, and it took me all these years to be brave to write this book, hoping I can save the life of some young man hiding in shame and full of dangerous thoughts and hatred.

As I was saying, the closer I got to her, the more confused I became. I was attracted to her, and at the same time, I was afraid of her! I wanted to drive by, and at the same time, if I didn't stop, I knew I might never see her again. Then I began to say to myself, "What if she rejects me? What if she sees the baggage I'm carrying, or at the same time, what if she doesn't reject me and realizes I'm different and wants to not hurry things because I can't perform like the other guys and she has to break through this wall. Is she patient enough, or will the slow interest in sex ruin the whole relationship?" I wanted her in my heart but not in my nature, which was usually the first response a man has when he meets a beautiful woman. But being abused sexually stops the heart from seeing the pleasure for the filth at first and puts building a meaningful relationship in slow motion, which requires a lot of patience from your partner, whether a male or a female.

But I must say attending church and reading my Bible on a somewhat regular basis seemed to give me more peace about myself and diminished the thought of me being abusive to others because of my pain, or should I say, because of trauma—which comes in many forms. Most people think that because you have been sexually abused, you will abuse someone in the same way, but for me, it was verbal and sometimes physical. And then on top of that, suffering from post-traumatic stress, I was a ticking time bomb.

As I stated earlier, I knew God did not want me to be the kind of person that I had become, so I relied heavily on Him because it seemed every day there was a reason for me to go off. But then I began to discover a very important issue—that my problem was, church was only compressing my anger and I felt like someone was sitting on me, someone that weighed a thousand pounds. I knew I needed someone to talk to, but who? At that time, the VA didn't care enough about veterans to give them means through which to seek help. Once you were discharged, you were on your own, and many vets ended up in prison. There really was no help there.

Getting back to my newly started relationship, the young lady and I began to see each other quite often and began to learn things about each other, and even though she had issues from a previous marriage and was several years younger than I was, we got along quite well. She had one child, and I had three. My three stayed with their mothers, and her child was with her. Since I loved children, it was not a problem for me. She was not a big cooker, so I did most of the cooking, which seemed to fit her daughter very well, because it was a change from fast food and breakfast cereal all the time. As time went on, we moved in together and began to use that word around each other—*love*. I really believe to this day that I loved her. She seemed to fit me very well. As a matter of fact, the first time we had sex, it was the bomb. Of course, that was the reason we had to be together all the time. Eventually, I asked her to marry me. My first wife and I had long parted and had been divorced for some time, and deep inside, I wanted to try to make up for the disaster that our marriage became somehow through this innocent person, who had nothing to do with the failure of that attempt of matrimony, to give me a second chance at perfection, when there was no attempt at healing the scars from the first fiasco I tried to endure.

Anyway, against all odds, we were married. We both did not want a church wedding; neither did we want a big one, so we decided the place where we were both comfortable at would do—her apartment. It was as good a place as any. To make a long story short, the first year was the best year, as in any marriage. I'm told they usually are! She worked, and we made plans to buy a home using my GI plan. So we started on a journey I thought was quite promising, and I felt quite secure in what we had done and in our life together. We both worked in a factory. As a matter of fact, they were a couple of blocks from each other, and I could drop her off, which was perfect. She made as much money as I did and was not afraid to work overtime. I came home dirty, and so did she. We got off at the same, which allowed us to shower or bathe together, and I thought I was in marriage heaven.

What I really loved about her was, she wanted things that I also did. We wanted things that were different from everybody else's. For instance, when we bought a second car, we both saw a little Saab car called a Sonnet, and we were sure no black person in town had one. Plus, it was great for gas and made us look very prosperous. Oh yes, as I mentioned before, she had a daughter, whom I absolutely adored. She was the most respectful child I had ever met, and I protected her with all I had from being hurt in any kind of way. She had buckteeth from sucking her thumb, and she was shy from being teased by others, even in her own family, sometimes by her mom. I was often mad at her mom for the names that she called her. One in particular was "my little monkey," and the bad thing about it was, the daughter favored her mother, so she was essentially calling herself names. I think that was one of the things that began to drive a wedge between us, because she knew I hated what she was doing. But with me being a man, and given the fact that we never talked about it, she never knew why. That it was my own abuse, it made me so angry.

Men, please hear me. This is why it's so important to get help. No one knows you need help if you don't talk. You can't get help if you don't ask. In my day, there was no help, but now after all the sexual abuse, rape, murder, physical abuse, PTSD in veterans, and much more, the country has finally started to take steps toward helping. It's not perfect, but it's a start. And further in my story, you'll see how important it is. I am asking all those that have never suffered from any abuse to not judge me by what I'm about to reveal, because it is very hard for me, but in order for you to understand, it must be revealed.

Back to the marriage. Through it all, we seemed to manage. I seemed to suppress my feelings, and we finally bought a house. Since we were the first blacks on the block, my wife was in a state of "black supremacy." We stayed among the white folks, and another one of her dreams had come true even though she never realized the toll it took on me. She wanted the house a different color, so since we couldn't hire anyone, it was all on me. After eight hours of work, I came home to paint the house. She was nice enough to have everything prepared for me to start when I got home. After the house was done, she wanted a new kitchen floor and bathrooms and whatever came to her mind. She loved decorating and was very good at it. At first, I was all in and felt very proud of all we had accomplished, but it seemed to never end. I started to lose sense of the fact that we were both in this together. All I did was try to make someone else happy and doing things I didn't even care about. This had nothing to do with what made me happy. It was all about her. I did not realize that it wasn't her but my sense of being secure in the relationship, being taken advantage of and manipulated, being used by the power of sex, being closed up in a dark place.

I began to strike out at her for everything she said or did. Trust went out the window. Why should I trust her when all she wanted to do was take me to the closet and use me in any way she felt wanted? At that time, it seemed like everything I did was because she wanted to keep up with her friends and others in her family that had gotten stuff in a ten- or fifteen-year span. She wanted it all at once. I did not know that this was probably what most women wanted—to let others see that she made the right choice in whom she chose as a mate, someone who could provide for her and was concerned about her happiness.

There's a song that I hear every now and then that says, "I wish I knew then what I know now." The next few years were not good. I knew something was wrong with me, so I went to talk to an old girlfriend of mine, seeking help, forgetting that our history wasn't too good either to the point where I had cheated on her. What was I expecting to get from her? It was like trying to give a bone to a rabid dog. What was I thinking?

Needless to say, the marriage was ripped apart. My physical and verbal abuse became too much for her to bare. I recall the last time the police were called, and we went to court. The police told her that if I touched her or even came close to her, she should get a gun and just kill me. I was not someone who should be living, let alone be a husband. Now the marriage was over. I was so angry and caught up in my own hurt and pain that I couldn't understand what I had done to her. I was so glad it was over. I gave her almost everything, figuring it wasn't paid for anyway. I thought, as a punishment, I would make her pay for it all.

After the divorce, I began to hang out on the weekends because I had to work and my job was my best friend. I was making pretty good money, so I became very independent and popular among the street ladies. Being a sharp dresser added to my popularity, so I started to go to strip joints and saw that the girls were attracted to my personality. Then I began to notice the pimps and players and thought this life would suit me fine since I had no one but myself to worry about.

Plus, I found out something that became very important to me. I could relate to them. Most were open and honest. We could talk about anything. They seemed to be able to open up and were real about who they were and why they chose that life. On top of that, they made plenty of cash—some from dancing and some from turning tricks. As time went by, I began to learn more and more about most of them, and most of them were surprised that I was not interested in sex. I just liked to hang out and go to breakfast after they got off, which was usually three or four in the morning. But most of them would talk about their life growing up and how it was cut short by some kind of abuse, mostly sexual. I mean, this was from being raped—some were raped by strangers, some by their uncles, and even some by their fathers. Some were even used by their parents to make money, and they weren't even in high school. But what hurt them the most was what kind of person they had become because of it. Like me, they hated themselves and everybody else.

Also at this time, I was staying with a young lady who would later become the mother of one of my children, a very sweet and loving person. She worked a nine to five at one of the prestigious colleges in South Bend but did what she had to do to make ends meet (if you know what I mean), but we got along quite well.

I remember one particular day we were home, and she wanted to visit a family member. I let her use my brand-new Buick to go visit, but on the way back, she totaled the car. Luckily, neither she nor her kids were hurt, but this accident was a godsend on my behalf—if you want to use that term in a non-godly lifestyle. Anyway, I got paid for the car, and on my way home from work, in a cab, I spotted a beautiful ivory Mercedes-Benz on the car lot. This was the year of 1979, and the car was 1969, chrome everywhere. Some thought it was a Rolls-Royce. It was a beautiful car, and since I was the first so-called player or pimp to have a car like this, I was the talk of the town. I exit the club and see people taking pictures with it, leaning or sitting on the hood. I was the bomb (or so I thought).

Now keep in mind that I had a job. I did not call myself a pimp or a player, but I wanted to have that reputation; at this time, I had about three girls in my so-called stable, and the only reason they were there was, most of the money they gave me I gave back to take care of their children. Also, since I had taken a class in accounting, I knew a little about finances and ran the game like a business, and it gave them some clout among the other women and made their pimps jealous.

But what really made then angry, besides having the car, was, I had managed to pull one of the prettiest girls in town, and the way it happened was purely just a happenstance. I happened to be on a street I normally did not go on. As a matter of fact, it was not even on that side of town. It was called "the lake," although there was no lake, just a little tributary body of water that was more like a pond or a swamp. But that's what they called it, so that's what it was as far as I was concerned. Anyway, on this particular day, it was raining hard and was not the type of weather to be out in. As I turned the corner on this street, I spotted a young lady walking in the rain. It was raining so hard I couldn't be sure, but it looked to me like she was crying. So I stopped to ask her if she needed some assistance in any way. She said no, but I could tell something was drastically wrong.

Now here I had my window down. It was raining so hard my car was getting wet on the inside, and so was I. so again I asked her if there was anything I could do. I took out my driver's license and let her see I meant no harm. After being drenched in the rain, she finally said she was on her way to get diapers for her children, and that struck a chord with me because God knows how I feel about children. The devil did also. But I convinced her to let me take her to the store, and she began to relax. I could see she was quite young. She was only eighteen and already had two children and was having a hard time. I also could see how beautiful she was, so I offered to help her with her problem and said that I would buy her whatever she needed. Then she got very defensive and replied that she was not going to do anything for money. I assured her that I was not that kind of guy.

After she purchased what she wanted, I told her that if she ever needed me, she could just call. She then replied, "With this car and your looks, I know you have another woman." I was honest and let her know that I did live by myself, which was true at the time. As a matter of fact, I had just moved into a three-bedroom home. So I gave her my phone number, still just wanting to help because she was so young and I had children her age or older. I only wanted to help, and I told her that was my only intention. I let her know that if she ever needed help or wanted to talk, she could call me. As for me, I was thirty-six and did not want a child as a woman, forgetting that in a sense she was not a child but a young woman with two children to care for.

As the weeks went by, I thought about her from time to time and hoped she was doing well. But one particular Friday, I had just gotten home from work and was taking a nap before I ate dinner when my phone rang, and it was her. She asked me if I meant what I said, that if she ever needed me, she could call. I replied yes. Then she said she and the children wanted to get away from her parents for a while. She asked if she could come over. After I thought about it for a few seconds, I said, "Fine." Then she asked me to come and pick them up, so I did. Needless to say, that weekend started a thirteen-year off-and-on relationship and resulted in my two sons, whom I raised as a single father after we split up. She was one of the very few women I actually fell in love with, and because of her and because they didn't understand why they could not get her, I became hated and despised by all of them.

I ended up getting jumped one night by about five guys. I was in the hospital for about three days, with cracked ribs, a broken nose, and other stuff. But all in all, I learned a valuable lesson about street people. They were not going to stop the game because you fell off, not a visit or a phone call; life must go on no matter what. And life did go on. I soon got well and got over it. It's one thing about abused people—they are tough and thick-skinned. There's not much that will keep them down, because they spend most of their lives trying to prove their worth, even though most of the time it was in the wrong way and they end up hurting others with their abuse.

I ended up moving to Virginia. I got a job running a fast food chain, got robbed and shot, ended up being a single father. Things were not working out, so I sent the children back to Indiana and moved to Ohio. That was where my life took a dramatic change. But what I failed to mention was, while in Virginia

I started using crack cocaine, thinking that would be the cure for my problems. Weed was just a pleasure, and I needed something that would make me forget the miserable forty-nine years of my life. I was too much of a coward to commit suicide and would rather someone else did the job for me, but God wasn't about to let that happen either. I'll save that story for later. But after passing the full-length mirror in my house and seeing myself about as big around as a toothpick, something began to talk to me. Satan tried to get me to see myself as I looked in the mirror, but God began to speak, and when God speaks, everybody and everything listens. He reminded me that He made me better than the picture Satan was painting of me.

I can remember this as though it were yesterday. The day that this dramatic change came about was on a Friday morning, at about 3:00 a.m., and I was just done smoking my last bit of crack cocaine, not knowing that it would really be the last time I put the pipe to my mouth. I began to pray and call on the name of Jesus, not only to heal me but also to rid me of this dependence on this evil god that I had chosen to deliver me of the past. And what I perceived to be the Holy Spirit began to bombard me with pictures of things that had happened to me from the beginning of my life and the things I had done to others because of those things, but one of the most dramatic sessions in all this was when it said I was forgiven and I was to forgive and that if I didn't stop what I was doing to myself, I was going to die. God had a purpose for me, and if I wasn't going to serve His purpose, what was the reason for me to live?

I don't know how quickly this all took place or how fast I reacted, but the first thing I knew was, I was throwing the crack pipe out the front door. I heard it break into pieces as it hit the concrete. It represented the broken pieces of my life being destroyed, and when the smoke cleared, I could not feel any of the effects of that demon in my body. I felt as if I had never smoked at all. I went into the bedroom and began to pack my clothes. There was one thing I was good at, and that was always having money. I would never smoke up my last. For some reason, I had a hidden pride and never wanted anyone to think I was a bum on crack, not even knowing how to manage my money. That's exactly what I was. Nevertheless, I had about $800 that was hidden from the woman I lived with at the time, because she had her issues also and she was a little weaker than I was. So I had to hide my money. But this is not to condemn her, because even in her state, she was a friend and a comfort. Besides, I knew she would be out all night with her gay friends, so I had plenty of time to pack my things.

It had to be about 6:00 a.m. when I finished packing, and being exhausted, I fell asleep and woke up at about 9:00 a.m. Still in full gear and revived, I headed for the U-Haul place and got a truck and took the furniture that was mine, which was most of it. I did leave her one of the beds. We had purchased the house together, and since she made the down payment, I thought it was only right she should have it. I wanted to leave behind everything that would weigh me down. But out of love and respect, I did go by her job to say "So long," and with me having a U-Haul and a car tow attached to the back, she had to know this was goodbye.

As I pulled up to the drive-through window, she put her head outside and held back the tears as we said our goodbyes to each other. I have often wondered about her, but I haven't seen her since. It's been about thirty years ago.

Well, here I was back on another journey, as my son Richard use to say, to find myself. By this time, I was breaking the age of forty-five or forty-six. In a black man's life, it's not too usual to not have a stable foundation because it seems you're always fighting the system to get treated fairly and you get used to being said so. Time seems to be on the side of those that are holding you back. Then sometimes you get the feeling God is punishing you for the personal choices you have made.

So there I was on the highway and really not going anywhere, because I really had nowhere to go. I thought about turning around, telling myself that it was the drugs and that if I left them alone I could still make it there. And by the time that thought vanished into the mist, I was about two hundred miles from where I left. Tears were rolling down my face for about the third time in my life. The first time, I was in a car wreck in California, and the second time was leaving my children's mother back in Indiana, going to Virginia. I cried all the way, which seems impossible but very true. I don't think I cried at all when I got shot. I guess the pain was too excruciating to cry.

But as Dolly Parton would say, "Here I go again." After a while, after gathering my manhood, I thought of going to Atlanta but decided to go to Ohio, where my sister was living. My mother was also there, as well as my younger brother. So I set my sights to Ohio, to which I believe God was leading me, and as you will soon read, after I got there, things began to change.

So I called my sister and told her I was on my way, and I think I gave her the indication I was coming to visit instead of staying for a while. I had no intentions of staying long, just until I got on my feet. Then after I got there, I found my younger brother had moved in too; now it was a real family affair. After about two or three weeks, with the help of my niece, I got a job at Chase Manhattan Mortgage, doing collections, which was new to me. It was such a cushy job, and there was no physical labor involved, though you had to have plenty of brain power. But I enjoyed it because I got a chance to wear a suit and tie and I had always dreamed of a job like that. It made me look important on the outside, covering up my past issues.

But before we get too far into my new job, let's back up a bit, because I must give God the glory. When I applied for the job at Chase, I was told that they would do an intensive background check that would take about two weeks, so being in trouble before, I kind of figured that job was not going to come. But I had begun to pray and read my Bible, and God had already begun to show up. I remember going to visit my uncle in Dayton, Ohio. He himself was a pastor, and my mother was a member of his church. On this particular Sunday, they were going visit another church, so I tagged along just to be with my mother since she seemed liked she was happy to be in my company. I don't know whether she knew what God had planned or if God just felt like showing up that day, but oh my Lord, what a day.

We arrived about 2:45 for the 3:00 p.m. service. I don't remember how or when the service started, but in the middle of the sermon the young man was preaching, there was something he said that God wanted me to hear. Tears began to fall. Sweat began to pour from my body. I could actually hear the moisture squishing in my shoes, as if I was walking on water. That was the day I believe my journey with Jesus really began. Oh, I know He had protected me all the years I had been living, but this was different; this was the day when I felt forgiven for all the wrong I had done, the day I knew what Jesus really died for. And that was me!

Not only was I forgiven for what I had done to others, but others were forgiven for what they had done to me. All the hate and the pain were washed away that Sunday afternoon. This is the day I believe Jesus said, "Drop your net, and follow me!" He said, "Drop all the dirt and the filth that got caught right along with the fish." In Matthew 11:28–30, Jesus said, "Come unto me all ye that labor and are heavy laden and I will give you rest." That day, all that I was carrying seemed to be lifted off my shoulders. I felt as if God had created that Sunday just for me. And when you continue reading, you will understand what I mean by the title of this chapter: "Salvation Brings Life."

If you will recall, I mentioned I had gotten the job at Chase Manhattan Mortgage. At the time, they were hiring account managers in the Accounting Department. I had received a phone call from them saying I was one of those people they hired, and they gave me a two-week starting date. In between that time, I would receive a letter with all the details concerning the position and what I had to do and the training that would be connected in performing the job. Well, the letter came about three to four days after I received the phone call. As I began to read the letter and all the requirements for the job, I ran across something that almost washed out my hopes in maintaining or keeping the job after being hired—there was a thirty-day trial period to see if a person was qualified for the position. And what scared me was, I had never used a computer. Yes, I had used a computerized cash machine, which consisted of putting in the numbers; it did the rest and sent the report to the main office. But that was small potatoes compared to what I was reading.

Now I want everyone reading this book to understand that this is not a book about religion; it's a book about faith. The devil doesn't come to destroy your religion; he comes to kill your faith. He knows your faith is what pleases God, and that is the last thing he wants to happen—that is, for you to please God.

Anyway, fear struck, and I started to worry, because I knew nothing about a spreadsheet or any of the requirements it took to do this job I was hired for.

But then the Spirit began to talk to me and said to me, "Stop worrying because for one thing, there was something they saw on your application that caused them to hire you. That is a plus. They offered training, and that is a plus." And then He said something that calmed all my fears, and that was, "And I'll be with you." People, that said it all. I knew by what was beginning to take place that I was not alone, and to explain that statement, let's regress for a moment. After my encounter with the Holy Spirit that Sunday, I was so excited about the new job I forgot my car was not operational. The transmission had stopped working because as I was coming from Richmond, Virginia, to Columbus, Ohio, which is a distance of almost five hundred miles, my car was hooked on a tow trailer behind the U-Haul truck but somehow it was not properly done and it ruined the transmission. Well, in reading the instruction manual, I found a clause that said a person from the U- Haul company was to give instructions on the proper use in mounting the vehicle to the trailer, which I did not receive. So after finding out about their blunder, I contacted them to see what could be done about my car and was told flatly nothing could be done. I even contacted a lawyer and was told the allegation would be hard to prove even though it was written down.

I had called the corporation's headquarters several times, and getting nowhere, I was sitting in my bedroom on the last Sunday before I had to start and thinking that I had no transportation of my own. Of course, my niece worked for Chase also, and I knew I could get a ride. But as the old saying goes, there's nothing like your own. While sitting on my bed, trying to figure out whether I would attend church that Sunday, I began to pray, and after praying and deciding I would not attend church, I crawled back into bed and fell asleep. Again I want readers to know this is not a book about religion but about faith. That Monday morning, which was about two days before my training was to start (which would be that Wednesday), I got up about 8:00 a.m., still frustrated about my dilemma. Something told me to call the U-Haul corporate office one more time. Well, as I was sitting there, wondering if this voice I was hearing was just my own attempt to work off my disappointment and lack of faith, the voice said to me again, "Call the corporate office." So against all that was in me, I picked up the phone, and after it rang several times, the urge to hang up was building. Then someone answered the phone, and I will never forget that voice or his name.

He said, "U-Haul corporate office. This is Jerry speaking."

I explained my problem to him, and the entire time, he listened very patiently. When I was done talking, he said, "Okay, Mr. Blake, let me see what I can do."

To make a long story short, he returned to the phone about twenty minutes later, which to me seemed like two hours, and said "Okay, Mr. Blake, take your car to the mechanic of your choice and have them call me personally."

I will just end this by saying what a praise party I had in that room!

Now this was just the very beginning of how my life began to change, though not without some challenges along the way. I recall about two months into my job, a friend and I were having lunch at a shopping mall across the street from the Chase building. On our way out the door, I realized by the excitement of the people that something was going on, so I began to look around to see if I could spot what or who was causing the commotion. I spotted this tall white man that everyone seemed to know but me, so I asked my friend who this person was. He told me he was a famous TV minister of a megachurch in Columbus, Ohio. Well, enough said.

In my mind, I thought, "Another money-hungry preacher." And I started to proceed to the exit. But before I could turn around good, this tall gentleman was in my face.

Against the caution of his security detail, he came over and placed his hand around my shoulders and said, "You have been carrying something inside for a long time. I just want to tell you God has lifted it. Now he has work for you to do." He then invited me to come visit his church.

I wondered why he didn't invite my friend, and I found out he was the cameraman for this church. Anyway, I went to one of his services and was greatly surprised by what I saw and felt. I ended up there for over two years and was greatly blessed. As a matter of fact, I invited a young lady there that was hooked on crack, and she was delivered. Twenty years later, she is still free from drugs, and we are still friends. This TV preacher is still preaching.

As for me, I didn't quite know what he meant when he told me God had work for me to do, but as time went on, I began to realize He was preparing me for something. I didn't understand, but my faith in Him had become greater, and my test became harder and harder. I thought it was punishment for things I had done, but I found out later He was building my strength and my character to fit His purpose.

CHAPTER 8

GOD'S PRESENCE

In this next chapter, my goal is to get those that are carrying the scars of some kind of abuse, especially from childhood, to know that with God's help, you can break the chain of any kind of abuse you may have in your life. As a matter of fact, life itself seems like one big episode of abuse one after another, whether it's sexual, physical, or verbal. Even racism is a form of abuse. Prison is a form of abuse. Anything that lowers a person's self-esteem and destroys a person's self-worth is abuse, especially by another person. And the younger you are, the heavier the baggage becomes. You begin to abuse others and can't understand why, and sometimes you can't even remember the moment the abuse occurred or when it took place. And since I am no doctor, I can only speak from experience, not from anybody else's experience, but from my own destruction of my life and others' lives I've touched.

Now I don't claim to be a great theologian or the most righteous, and sometimes I don't even know why Christ even chose me to carry His message. And for many years, I ran from His voice because I felt ashamed and not worthy of His grace for me to even associate my name with His. But I found that when Jesus calls you, He calls you by the name you hate, and when you accept Him, He changes your name to one that can be remembered for His glory. I hope I can control myself while I'm trying to write this chapter because it is all about Him, and when I begin to talk about Him, it is like having your finger on the button controlling a nuclear weapon. You just want to set it off, and I mean that in a good way. It was like fire in Jeremiah's bones, but it's like dynamite shut up in mine, because His presence is just that powerful.

But let me get on with my story. As you can remember, I've mentioned my car being fixed—the job with Chase. And by the way, I ended up being the employee of the month, and even though racism and hate cause me to leave that job, Jesus began to do great things in my life. After two years on the job and a blessed two years at World Harvest Church under a great pastor (without his permission, I won't mention his name), I moved to a place I've always wanted to live in. By this time, I was a single father and had custody of my two sons. We were on our way to a new life in Atlanta, Georgia! Well, when we arrived, I remember it rained for about two weeks straight, and I was out looking for a job. We were living in a one-bedroom unit at an extended-stay motel. They had the bed, and I had the let-out sofa, but I was feeling like I was at a thousand-dollar-night hotel. It was so peaceful and quiet, and I knew God was in control of our situation and that everything was going to be fine.

I finally got a job at a call center and got my oldest son in school. My youngest was not old enough, so I found him a sitter after really scrutinizing her for weeks. After what happened to me, it was very hard for me to trust anyone with him. But she worked out okay. As a matter of fact, she had a son the same age, and they became very good friends. Life was good thus far. I found a great church, and I was chosen as the deacon in charge. I was struttin' my stuff, but little did I know that when you think you've got it made, God will test you or the devil will want to steal your faith.

After about five years on the job, I had bought another car from a Buy Here, Pay Here car dealership. The car I came from Ohio retired itself and left me stranded, but again God was faithful. I had rented a three- bedroom apartment, and the three of us were having the time of our lives. Or at least they were. Now I know that what I'm going to say next some people won't believe, but this is true and may kind of put my manhood to a test. But I must be truthful in order for people to get the full effect of this book.

At this time in my life, I was about fifty-nine and began to feel lonely, and after walking around, I was seeing other couples that seemed to be happy—you know, in the stores and at the mall. They were laughing and smiling, having fun, and there I was, alone and not feeling complete, afraid to even take a chance on love. The most unbelievable part was, I had had no companionship or sex for years, and like I've said before, I do not have a gay bone in my body. My oldest son used to say, "Dad, why don't you go out on a date and have some fun? You're always at home." He would introduce me to some of his friends' mothers, and every now and then, I would go out but never a second time. The women could not figure out why this well-dressed, handsome man never called back.

The funniest thing was, when I heard other men talking about their sexual encounters and being so enthused over what they experienced, it never even fazed me. Oh yeah, I would laugh along with them, but they had no idea of my real thoughts. I was active in church, and that became my life, so it never really bothered me the least bit. As a matter of fact, I knew plenty of women wanted me—some my age and plenty younger than me—and I began to take pride in the fact that I had that effect on them.

I had joined another church. I was licensed as a minister and now ordained as an elder and was not going to let anyone or anything ruin my relationship between God and myself. He had been so very kind to me. Even though I wanted a woman and a relationship, God knew my condition was very fragile, and He protected me and gave me strength to resist any temptation that came before me—and it was a lot.

People don't understand, as I didn't at the time, that the church is full because it's full of those that have been hurt or abused in some manner, seeking help from anger and shame of something they have done or whatever was done to them, sometimes both. They don't know that just going to church on Sunday helps but that it's not the only cure, because it's when you are not at church that you really need someone to talk to. As time went by, I began to study God's Word more and more, and He opened my eyes more and more. I began to preach, and the power in His Word started healing those around me just as it had healed me. People began to gravitate toward me, especially women, and being single, it was very hard for me to find a balance between them seeking the love of God and the expectations they had of me.

My pastor was married. They knew his counseling was only under the confines of another person such as a Deacon or an assistant Minister, and his wife person would also know their business. But for me, I was not attached to anyone at the time, and it seemed easier to come to me. The devil would use this position to destroy my relationship with God, but by His grace, I was able to resist. This also got me in trouble because the women either thought I was uppity and thought I was gay. They never said it to my face, but when you have been in a place as long as I had been and you never try to approach them with sexual favors, they found this unusual. They did not know that God was also protecting them from me, because I myself was damaged goods, and they did not know that their healing was also my healing.

As time went by, I reached my sixth year of membership, and God begin to tug at me about pastoring my own church. At first, just like Jonah, I said it will never happen. Well, telling God that was definitely the wrong thing to do! But I fought for about a year, acting like I didn't hear Him. He would wake me at two and three o'clock every morning, including times when I had to preach; my sermon would be dry as a bone. So after a year, I gave in, putting the ball back in His court, so to speak. I was making excuses, such as "Lord, you know I'm not married. Should I not have a wife first?" or "Where is the money going to come from to start a church?" and "Where am I going to start? In Atlanta, there is a church in every corner!"

Well, I decided to look for a wife among the congregation. I was very popular and could have my pick of the single ladies, and now at the age of sixty-three or somewhere about, I could have had anyone from thirty- five on up to fifty-five, which was my limit. People, if you think God does not have a sense of humor, just stand by! On one particular Sunday, the church had a special program, and this evangelist minister came to present a play and had five or six ladies with him. Now please pay attention. In this group was one very beautiful woman, at least to me; and as I was sitting there, it seemed like I heard the Spirit say, "She is going to be your wife." And mind you, I was sitting in the pulpit at the time. I said back to the Spirit, "Okay. I'm game. Now how are you going' do it?"

Now I'm going to blow your mind! About two Sundays later, she returned to do a puppet show, and on the third time, she was alone. As she did her puppet thing, I became more intrigued and really wanted to meet her, but she left before I could get to her. I was more convinced than ever that she was going to be my wife. She was beautiful, sexy, and most of all, a woman of God. That was the kicker. Field goal!

On that Wednesday night, at Bible study, I was in the office with the pastor and one of the deacons and began to explain what the Spirit had told me about this lovely lady. To my surprise, the deacon began to laugh, and the pastor had a look of "Not possible!" Then they began to explain she was already spoken for and was soon to be married. I met her one more time and approached her in the parking lot and asked if she had someone, and indeed, she did. She was to be married! But she also replied there was nothing written in stone, and I wondered what she meant by that. You will find out as we continue on. But she did get married and came to join our church and introduced her husband, and it was then that I said to my Spirit, "Stay out of my personal life." Why would God make me go through this, knowing my past and knowing my struggle?

After a year had passed, I was over that ordeal. As a matter of fact, I had my eye on a cute little Jamaican girl. The only thing that held me back from her was, she had two young children and I thought I might have become too old to deal with young children on an everyday basis. So that thought ended, and I was beginning to feel content that if I were to start a church, it would be alone.

Now, folks, hang on to your hats and garter belts. On one bright and sunshiny Sunday in July—I remember it very well—she showed up. Now remember, she and her husband had already joined, but this time, she was alone. She began to explain why she had not returned and that they were divorced and no longer together. I began to think all sorts of reasons as to why this beautiful woman would confess to the whole congregation about something most people would try to hide. It's one thing about being abused; it automatically puts you in a state of silent rage. In the state of feeling sorry for someone who has been hurt, you want to come to the rescue of that person and, on the other hand, to stay away because it is also a reminder of the past. You want to help, but why should you? You want to trust, but trust is hard to extend to another person, especially to a woman because you see her as not trustworthy and full of hidden secrets and schemes to get revenge or to have their way. And if you get into a relationship with that person, it will be like dodging bullets, only the bullets are the attacks of the pain and hurt caused by someone else's doing. Believe me, I know it very well. I had been on both ends of the spectrum.

So I still did not pursue this opportunity and ignored it because I was clear of most of the emotions that I had carried for years and those that hadn't completely gone, I had learn to control them. So while I prayed for her situation, I was glad it wasn't me. Well, to my surprise, that voice decided to show up again about three months after her announcement, and the funny thing is, all this time, I couldn't keep my eyes off her. There was something about her that intrigued me and aroused my curiosity, and it had went far beyond her looks or any sexual fantasy. I really began to like her.

Here it was Sunday again. Church service had just ended, and I saw her as she went out the door and headed for her car. I was sitting in the pulpit, mind you, after a very stirring and spiritual service. The voice came again, and this time it was louder than ever. It said to me that if I did not go after her, I would never have a chance to have her for my wife. Now, people, please listen. This was all in a few seconds. Sweat began to pour from my face, and a sense of urgency came over me like never before. I was convinced this was the Holy Spirit and that if it were, this was what God wanted for me. This was the person He knew I needed to carry out His purpose for me, and that was to build a church and become a pastor even if I truly didn't know why.

So out in the parking lot I went, and just as she was getting in her car, I called out to her. The funny thing is, I had avoided holding a conversation with most of the women at church because I didn't want anyone to think I was a womanizer. It was one of the things the pastor always reminded the single men of the church about, that they should not be dating women after women in that church. It was not acceptable!

But this day, I did not care who saw me, and on top of that, I was just acting on what I believed the Holy Spirit was saying to me and expected this to be a futile attempt at nothing. She heard me, and she rolled down her window. I introduced myself again as if she didn't know who I was, and she politely replied, "Oh, I know who you are!" Then I began to explain what I believed to be the voice of God had told me.

I began by saying, "Ma'am, you're going to think this is crazy, but God informed me you were going to be my wife." Boy, that went over well!

She laughed and replied, "Well, why didn't I get the memo too?"

That I couldn't answer and thought I had made a big fool of myself and was ready to end the foolishness I had caused. Then it felt like something or someone just took over my tongue, and I asked her if she was hungry.

She said, "Just a little. Why, are you going to take me to dinner?"

I then replied, "I will do you one better."

She replied, "What's that?"

I told her I had cooked a roast, and I invited her to dinner at my home. After convincing her I was safe and not a serial killer, she accepted. We talked and laughed and got to know each other as much as we could for a first date, if you want to call it that.

And as time went by, we went to a movie and out to dinner and met each other's children. My two boys were happy and were quite surprised she was as nice looking as she was for her age. I later found out she loved to exercise and keep in shape; she even convinced me to start taking better care of myself, and I began to thank God for putting this person in my life. Without a doubt, I knew it had to be Him.

And what was more convincing was what happened next as time went by. I met a gentleman who owned a few eating places and was getting ready to open another. He found out that I had managed a few restaurants in the past, and after meeting him, I started working in one of his already established one so he could work at the one he was opening at a new location. When it was up and running, he transferred me to the new location and wanted me to hire the staff I would need. Now this is another time I thought God was working out His promise to me. My wife-to-be had a son who was a very talented and inspiring chef and was not employed at the time, and I knew it was just a matter of time. I was being retired in the first place, so I would be leaving, and I wanted to leave my friend someone he could trust and knew what he was doing. So I hired him, and we became somewhat close.

As time went by, I began to confide in her son how I felt about his mother, and just when you think things are going in your favor, here came a snag. He was very resentful about my suggestion that I wanted to marry his mother. He stated he didn't care about us dating and that he would do everything he could to deter us from getting married. It wasn't until later that I understood why.

Suddenly, I was thrust into this arena of resentment and dislike because of the experience that her son suffered over her not being able to have a long-term relationship. I discovered she had been married a number of times—as a matter of fact, an unusual amount of times. As a matter of fact, so had I. She would be on number five, and I would be on number four. I soon realized for the first time, through the embarrassment that her son demonstrated, how my own children must feel. Please bear with me, folks. I know this book is primarily about abuse, and I have not forgotten. This segment is headed that way. For some reason, I have found out that abuse is the foundation of most people's (rather man or woman) mental breakdowns, and it does not matter what their status in life is.

This beautiful woman was a high school graduate and a college graduate, smart as a whip, and after having relationships with prostitutes and tricksters and hearing their confessions and understanding their assessment of life, I still could not understand why a man would not want to love a woman like this. After all, I was falling in love with her, and we hadn't even slept together, going on six months. But then again, I couldn't understand why a woman could not love a man like me, and I began to find out we had so much in common.

After analyzing and thinking about our relationship, I started to wonder if the reason God had put us together was the fact that we both shared a secret—a secret of abuse. Even though we had not discussed it between us, I figured by my own issues that somehow she was fighting the same demon as I was. Maybe she was my reflection even though she was female and I was male. It would be easy for us to form a relationship because we could understand each other's emotions and feelings. Maybe the other men in her life didn't take the time to understand what she was carrying inside and just looked at what they saw on the outside. Men do that, you know. Then my emotions all seemed to rise up at the same time. You've heard the song "Mixed Emotions"? Then I went into my protect mode. I wanted to make sure this beautiful creature would not be hurt again.

So after almost a year of courtship and against the advice of others (me, my mother, her mother, her sons), we got married. Now here's where it gets interesting! Neither one of us wanted a church wedding because we knew that due to our past, we would be judged by all those who didn't know how long we were dating and the holier than thou people who may have thought we were hiding the fact that we were having sex, which we were not doing because that was something we both insisted on. She did not want a diamond ring, which I would have very well bought her with no hesitation. We went to the justice of the peace, and that was fine since I've never had a church wedding anyway. We were married on my birthday, January 20, which in Indiana was usually the coldest day of the year. The Super Bowl and elections all happened on that day, and I was getting married, so I knew this was a special time for me.

Now, readers, please understand. This book is about the effects abuse has on children. Even though I am grown now—well in my early sixties—I was once a child, and the effects are lifelong. That's why it is so very important to protect your children and to get help right away if you suspect anything wrong. I'm putting myself on front street so you will know the signs. Life will already be a struggle, and there's just so much we can carry.

Now back to my story! Even though we had courted and there was a level of intimacy, like kissing and hugging, and I knew I loved her, in the back of my mind, I was afraid that I would not be able to perform sexually; even though I had children and sex was nothing new, it took a whole lot of passion for me to do my part. As I stated earlier, it was almost like having an erectile dysfunction, and all the time we were saying our vows, in the back of my mind, I was afraid! Without going into details, by the grace of God, everything worked wonderfully, and I knew more than ever that God had put us together. Then I began to think about another problem that would surely occur. Since I had such a low tolerance for sex and would probably not approach her for sex, would she think that was odd? I would always wait until my mate (whoever that was) was ready to have sex. Then I knew the passion would be there to arouse me. But one of the good things about our marriage was, even though she worked and I was retired, she was adamant about getting her rest and made it clear not to wake her in the middle of the night or early in the morning. That was fine with me because it let me off the hook and I did not have to explain my problem. But man, when we did have sex, whenever it was, it was great!

We were married for seven years. The first five was awesome. I would cook for her and clean up to make sure she had nothing much to do. She would not let me wash clothes or cook Sunday dinner. She could cook too, just like mom. We even built a ministry together. Then things began to fall apart. It really became stressful. Why? I really don't know. It wasn't because I didn't love her, and I do still to this day. I came to the conclusion that we were both damaged goods and we did the best we could to make it work. We still remain friends and hope the best for each other. She still does God's work. She loves children as I do, and I am still in the ministry also.

I was angry at God at first because I figured He orchestrated everything and I couldn't understand the reasoning behind the whole thing. But I know that if He did it, there has to be a reason, and I have learned not to question His motives. Since I had moved into her home since it was cheaper, I had given mine up. I had to start over once again, but since then, I have bought two homes— one for my sons and one for me. God continues to keep His promises.

CHAPTER 9

THE EFFECTS OF OPEN EYES

Well, readers, this is the last chapter and perhaps the shortest one. My children are all grown now and have children of their own. For the most part, they are all good parents—better than I was, as I was better than mine.

It is such a wonderful thing when God opens your eyes and shows you how all the wrong and sick parts of your life can be a healing for someone else if we only communicate.

It took me all these years to understand why so much happened to me and why so many things went wrong when I tried to do right. The Bible says God takes everything meant for evil and turn it for the good. We may not ever understand God's logic, and sometimes we get angry with Him. But I believe He picks out some of us to shine the light on certain things so we can become better human beings.

Yes, abuse in any form should be uncovered, but let us start at the roots instead of condemning others that commit these acts. And yes, they should be punished, but punish them with compassion, and make sure we provide the proper help. We lock people up and think that's the cure, but we're only trying to fix abuse by adding more abuse.

Abuse has been around since the beginning, and it has been in every culture. When I was in Vietnam, I would see a man get angry at his wife, and he would pick up a stick and beat her. She was not allowed to defend herself or even show any kind of emotion. But we are the leaders of the world, and we should set the example.

Abuse ruins lives. It lingers inside a person like cancer. The bad part is, once it's done to a child, it's with them forever. You may say, how can a four-year-old remember being abused? Well, I'm a witness, and the overwhelming effects are, they will abuse others also. You can count on it.

Abuse breeds hate, disrespect, and dishonor. It covers up love like snow covers the ground, and it hides deep within our soul. In my case, I can only thank God for my recovery because no one else could help or didn't know how. Even now, the effects of my abuse and what it did to my life makes me angry, because even though I'm blessed, I could have done so much more in life and could have not been plagued with the memory of those I hurt along the way.

And, men, if you're reading this, please go get help. Get rid of the baggage. You don't have to carry it like I did. Even though the woman that abused me has passed on, I never got a chance to confront her like so many has done today. As life went on, I began to realize that someone abused her so I forgave her, just as I forgave my father after I searched in his past and saw how he grew up. I don't think I would have made it as long as he did.

And, women, I urge you to please be passionate. Yes, abuse should be reported, and yes, the perpetrator should be punished. But don't use it as a tool of hatred. See it as a tool to bring about a change in our human behavior, not only for this country but for the world. It takes both men and women to keep the human race going, and if we hate each other, the world will soon die, which it is doing at a fast pace. It doesn't matter whether the abuse is from a man or a woman; it's not good.

In my case, being abused by a woman was considered a badge of honor by the men I sought help from. We can't see the trauma it causes because of our feeble-mindedness. And I do pray that we can change the face of our human existence and get back to loving one another.

THE END

About the Author

My name is Richard Earl Blake, also called by Richard Earl Underwood. Blake was my mother's maiden name.

I served in Vietnam as an infantryman in the USMC, and I was discharged with honor and now serve my community as a pastor.

Thank you in advance for reading this book. Please protect your babies because they are our future. To all my children, I thank God for you because without you, I don't know how I would have made it.

Giving much thanks to God gave me the courage to write this book.

God bless you all.

Richard E. Blake

www.ingramcontent.com/pod-product-compliance
Lightning Source LLC
Chambersburg PA
CBHW031224120626
46545CB00003B/977